"LITTLE GIRL'S STORY OF A SUPERHERO: A HEARTFELT TRIBUTE TO FATHERHOOD"

A STORY OF RESILIENCE, EMPOWERMENT AND AUTHENTICITY.

DR. VINUSHA VIJAYAKUMAR

In loving memory of my late father, M. C. Vijayakumar,
Your unwavering belief in my dreams and your enduring love
continue to guide me every step of the way. This book is dedicated
to you, a constant source of inspiration and strength.

Contents

Foreword

First and foremost, I thank Vinusha for giving me this opportunity to write the Foreword for her book, which she has written in memory of her father, who passed away unexpectedly, leaving her devastated. The author has described the remarkable personality of her friend, philosopher, guide, and mentor, her Dad, whom she calls her Superhero.

This is a fitting tribute to someone she respects, loves, and idolizes for being the caring, understanding, supportive, nurturing father _ her role model, and the shining beacon in her life. It is genuinely ennobling to read about the sacrifices a father can make for the well-being and education of his children to give them the best possible advantages in life, giving them all the support he had not enjoyed during his growing-up years.

The author describes in detail how she and her sister were brought up by her father. He was indulgent and gave his children everything, even before they asked for it, contrary to his austere upbringing. In the chapters devoted to her father's childhood, the author has related his special relationship with his mother. In later years, after achieving success in life, he fulfilled his duty of caring for his parents. In recounting details of life within a middle-class home, the author shows respect for family and traditions, which is so lacking in today's younger generation.

The book also offers many insights into the working of successful relationships within a family, particularly the beautiful husband-wife relationship that her parents shared. Talking about her father at his workplace, the author describes how much respect he showed his subordinates how easily he resolved conflicts, and despite being in a place of power, he never showed off. This is one of the author's many reasons for saying, "That's why my dad is a Superhero."

The author's writing style is very natural, flowing out of her thoughts. What comes through is the authenticity. There are also moments of extreme emotion, expressed beautifully, such as the performance of the last rites of her father.

I recommend reading this book because the author has given us a beautiful pen picture of a man who was the epitome of fatherhood and has also chronicled all the life lessons she has learned from him. This can serve as a valuable guide to living a life with integrity and coping with adversities in the face of all odds. I wish the author all success.

Dr. Roshmi Roy
Author and Transformational Coach

Preface

Prepare to embark on a heartfelt journey through the extraordinary life of the unsung hero of my world: my dad. While he might not have worn a cape or possessed superhuman abilities, his daily acts of courage and love painted the portrait of a genuine superhero in my eyes.

In the pages ahead, I'll unveil the moments that defined his resilience, the hurdles he overcame, and the unwavering love he showered upon us, crafting a life of abundance from seemingly meager beginnings. This book is a tribute to the magic woven by an ordinary man, proving that true heroism lies not in grand gestures but in the simple, unwavering dedication to those he holds dear.

Beyond a simple memoir, this tale serves as a guiding light for parents, an inspiration to nurture and protect, and a poignant reminder to daughters of the indelible imprint left by their fathers. So, fasten your seatbelts and get ready to immerse yourself in the enchanting chronicles of "Little Girl's Story of a Superhero."

Dr. Vinusha Vijayakumar

Acknowledgements

I am deeply grateful to everyone who has been instrumental in the creation of this book.

First and foremost, I would like to express my heartfelt appreciation to my mother, V. Malarkodi, whose unwavering inspiration continues to fuel my passion and dedication every day. My sister, Varsha, has been an incredible pillar of support, providing encouragement and actively contributing to the development of various chapters.

I extend my profound gratitude to my grandparents, Chandrasekar and Ambujambal, for instilling the values of perseverance and determination in us. I owe a debt of gratitude to my late grandmother, Pushpa Navaneethakrishnan, for her unwavering belief in my abilities and for imparting the invaluable lessons of discipline and resilience.

I am also grateful to my cousins, Mahesh Jaganathan, Sneha Sampath and Vishwajit Duraiarasan for their significant contributions to the various chapters of this book. My heartfelt thanks to Michelle Salve for conceptualizing the captivating book cover and to Rakshanda Rashid for the artistic design that brought the book's essence to life. I sincerely thank Dr. Roshmi Roy for graciously crafting the foreword that sets the tone for this work. Special thanks to my niece, Dhanya MS, for her unconditional love and infectious energy that were crucial in executing my ideas.

I sincerely appreciate my family, friends, colleagues, mentors, and fellow coaches' unwavering support and belief in my abilities. Your encouragement has been invaluable throughout this journey, and I am truly grateful for your continued presence and guidance.

Thank you all for being an integral part of this incredible journey.

Dr. Vinusha Vijayakumar

Prologue

The phone call that changed everything arrived on a quiet Thursday morning; as I listened to the solemn voice on the other end, my world suddenly stopped. "Your dad is no more," the words echoed in my mind, each syllable carrying the weight of a lifetime of memories and unspoken love.

At that moment, time seemed to collapse, and I found myself suspended between the fragments of a once-lived life and the unfathomable reality of a world without my dad. Amidst the chaos of emotions, a steadfast resolve took root, urging me to embark on a poignant journey back to the place I once called home, where the fragrance of childhood memories still lingered.

As I boarded the flight that would carry me back, fragments of the past came flooding back, painting vivid portraits of a life enriched by the unwavering presence of a man who had been my beacon of strength. Memories of laughter shared, lessons learned, and unspoken affection enveloped me, intertwining with the rhythmic clatter of the train tracks beneath me.

The journey homeward bore the weight of a lifetime's worth of moments, etched in the fabric of my very being. It was a voyage to bid farewell to a beloved father and celebrate a life that had touched countless souls with its warmth and kindness. With each passing mile, I found myself retracing the footsteps of a life well-lived, brimming with the wisdom of a man whose legacy would forever be engraved in the tapestry of my existence.

Join me as I traverse the corridors of time, reliving the cherished moments and unspoken truths that shaped the Little Girl's Story of a Superhero. This tale transcends the boundaries of loss and celebrates the enduring legacy of a father's love.

ONE

THE LIFE-CHANGING PHONE CALL

One bright morning when the sun was shining so brightly while I was jogging, I received messages from the school principal and other teachers wishing me on doctor's day; it seemed to start quite like a happy and beautiful day filled with positivity when I had no clue what this day was about to bring.

I was working as a medical officer for an international school in the neighbouring state. Like any typical day, I remember walking through the garden of my workplace, cherishing all the beautiful wishes I received that day while walking from my boarding house to my clinic, replying to the most special message from Dad, saying, "Thank you, Dad." I also forwarded to our family group the personalized message sent on doctor's day, and I know my dad would have felt thrilled and proud seeing it.

The night before, I spoke to my dad; he told me to enquire about an online job. I enquired and told my dad it was a scam, but his voice seemed slightly disappointed. I asked him, "Don't you like your current job?" he replied, "No, no, not like that; it is just that I wanted to do something additional, a part-time job like your prescription verification job." Then, half an hour later, I video-called him as usual, but he refused to talk to me, saying he was tired. I felt awful as my dad had never declined to speak to me before, but I didn't disturb him; looking back, his health was deteriorating, and he didn't want me to get bothered about it as I was far away from home.

As I started the usual work of the clinic, checking screening records for that day and texting my other doctor friends wishing them, I received a phone call from my elder sister with a terrified voice saying, "Call daddy's office; it seems dad has fainted." I was frozen for a second, barely able to process the thought. I can't express my panic while sitting in the infirmary. Slowly, I moved out; I walked down the corridor back to the garden, trying to comprehend the situation with all kinds of confused thoughts, "What could have possibly happened? "Could it be an accident?" "Is he stable?", "How do I treat him from here ?" and a million other questions cropped up in my mind. I had never been in such a state of panic, so frozen that I couldn't even decide how to proceed. My sister forwarded me another number from my dad's office to enquire about the scenario.

I called my dad's office; his work colleague said agitatedly, "Your dad is being seen by the doctor." I heaved sigh of relief as I thought he was getting some medical help. I called two colleagues back in my hometown to check on him as I was miles away. One of my colleagues was on his way to my dad's office; I was numbed and lost in my thoughts. I got a phone call from another friend with whom I shared everything. Suddenly, for a second, I felt an unusual feeling of intense peace and silence among all the chaos happening, which is totally contradictory to what I was feeling a moment ago; I felt my dad's presence several minutes before I had an official call saying that he was no more. I have read about telepathy and heard from people's experiences, even of my mom, but it was the first time ever I felt another person's presence in their physical absence. That moment of intense bliss freaked me out, knowing something unusual and unexpected was on my way. At this moment, knowing what all this meant, I couldn't put it into words or was confused about how to deliver this news to the management and go back home.

Here comes the third call from my sister, asking if I had contacted the office; I replied that I needed to book a ticket and fly back home. This was all before I received an official call announcing his death. With a broken heart, my sister gets disappointed in me and says, "Why do you talk like that?" and cuts the call. I was as broken as she was, but I don't know where I got the courage to have such a life-changing conversation without emotionally breaking down. All I could think of was God; I sat down for meditation in that crucial situation, sending pure feelings and good wishes to my dad and my family members, who may be deeply saddened by the news. I don't even understand, up to this day, how I faced the entire situation with so much poise and calm without breaking down. A few minutes later, I got the final call from my sister saying that " My dad had passed away" after an official confirmation from a nearby hospital.

That news, which I realized a few minutes ago, turned into a reality; my heart felt so much pain, as if it was being entirely ripped up, that I had lost the gold while in search of pearls that I didn't have anything valuable left in my world, the feeling of betrayal as how my dad so close and near to me couldn't wait for me to give me a chance to say the final goodbye and to say how much I loved him, how I sat there as i saw the pillar of my entire dream life shattered, feeling absolutely not interested in anything about this cruel meaningless life without my dad. My immediate thoughts shifted from my dad to other family members as to how they would handle this, even when a person like me, who has been practicing meditation for years and understands how to take God's help in challenging situations, was stumbling with overwhelming emotions.

Surprisingly, it was so weird that contrary to the turmoil inside my head, I could barely cry, thinking only of what needed to be done next. I met my reporting authority, informing him that I needed to go back home. My reporting authority asked me, "What has happened ?" I couldn't say a word and was frozen for a minute or so again; the director asked me, "Come on, speak up, mam." Some broken sentences came out of my mouth along with some overwhelming emotions: " I want to go back home. My dad is no more," the director convinces me, saying, "Nothing would have happened to him, he would be alright, our office would help you book a ticket. " I also had the right kind of support around me at that time who helped me stay calm and helped me in all ways possible.

As I walked from my clinic to my boarding house, I was totally broken; my heart felt heavy, like something I had never experienced before. I held myself together without crying until I reached my boarding house. On the way, I saw many school employees wishing me good morning and asking if I would have tea; I just said, Good morning, and I have some work, bye and hurriedly rushed into my room. Every moment of that day is still crystal clear in my head. I locked my room. I tried to let out the sorrow by crying, but I could barely call. I can't even bear the emotional scenes of separation between a dad and daughter shown on the television; tears would flow down my cheek as if it were happening to me. I could barely cope when someone said that my dad was not mine, even joking; now I am here absolutely knowing that I have lost him forever, can't talk to him, can't enjoy and share good times with him, nor hold his hand when I am really in a stressful situation, I couldn't feel sorrow or any feelings for that matter.

I came to my apartment and sat on the balcony, staring at the garden below; I couldn't process anything about what happened. My cousin called to check on me and talk about my dad; I could cry now and couldn't speak a word back except I knew. Every time anyone close to me, I felt a massive wave of sorrow ripping my heart apart. The nurse working in my clinic followed me into my room, convincing me that everything would be alright. Enquiring what had happened, I said calmly in an agitated voice and very confused that my dad was no more, and I gave her my debit card to bring to the office to book my return ticket. She and the office people helped me process the flight ticket back to my home, and she cooked rice vermicelli for me, telling me to eat; I couldn't eat or think straight, deeply saddened packing the necessary stuff, I had to wait an hour or so before we started to the airport. As I walked from my room to the gate, I never saw anyone in the eye; I felt like I had Nothing valuable left in my life. The school vehicle took us from the school to the airport, and the sister from the infirmary there accompanied me.

I got all my cousins and relative's calls one by one; at this moment, every time I picked up a call from someone close to me, like my cousin, brother, or sister, I finally cried and expressed my sorrow, not knowing what to reply except for "I know, and I am coming home, please take care of my mom till I reach there." On my way to the airport, 40 kilometres away from my workplace, I got a message of my dad's picture lying in the hall of my hometown. I saw him lying in the cold box in his violet checked shirt, with mouth a little open stuffed with some *tulsi*, eyes closed, and a black shadow under his eye indicating his lifelessness. I felt totally broken and couldn't stop the tears from flowing down my eyes. I was angry that my dad hadn't waited for me to say his final goodbye; I was thinking how unfair it was for life not to give me a chance to ask him what was the last thing that he wanted. For a moment, I realized that he wouldn't have had any idea it was to happen to him, and my anger quickly dissolved as my love for him was more massive than mine. That travel to the airport seemed longer. I wanted to return home immediately and take charge of the situation. I saw a quote on the way, "Avoid bad company." For some reason, it struck me hard and felt like a final message from my dad.

The school vehicle arrived at the airport. It was a totally unfamiliar place with an unknown language, and I walked into the airport, showing my ticket and identity card. There were strict COVID precautions. I had so much pain, but I couldn't even shed a tear as I didn't want to disturb other people's peace around me in the airport. I saw different families with kids, some business people, and friends all waiting for their flight. For the first time ever,

I realized not all air travel was happy; previously, air travel meant for me that I came home, and it was a comfortable place for me. I wondered how many people around me may have untold sorrow behind their ordinary casual looks just like me, and I felt mercy for them. As I got inside the airport after finishing my formalities, I was waiting for my boarding call; I was all alone, and that time allowed me to rethink and evaluate the decisions I had taken in my life and their impacts on my family, I was left with the realization that time with my loved ones is not forever, how blind and self -centred I have thought I will do the best of the things and create beautiful memories with my family maybe 10 years down the line once I have settled in my career. However harsh the reality may be, I had to face the truth and the consequences of my false understanding of life.

This decisive event subsequently changed all my life decisions and attitude towards life. For anyone reading this book right now, pick up the phone, tell your loved ones how much you love them, make time to visit them, and make them a priority long before you are put in a situation like mine where I can do nothing except have regret. Most valuable things in life don't come with a price tag but with a time tag, especially when it comes to the people we love. That was also the day I realized sometimes it really requires painful events to enhance our perception of the beautiful life we all take for granted, and it is also nature's way of teaching us a life lesson.

God had given us the ability to form and recall memories; maybe he knew that it could help heal one's seemingly unrepairable broken parts of the heart. All I had left now was the memory of the beautiful times I spent with my dad, and I started recalling all the events from my past; everything felt so vivid and clear. For some time, I fell asleep, felt totally deported to the past, and woke up hearing the boarding call of my flight. For some reason, the seat next to me was empty, but I felt my dad's presence and company all throughout my journey. I couldn't shed a tear during this time, knowing that my dad may be observing me silently and that if I cried, it would break his heart and drown him.

We have all heard the phrase "the power of regret," and it exists. It can be hard to move on after a loved one dies, but if you let your memories consume you, you might never heal. It is important to remember the good things that happened in your life and the memories you shared with the person who passed away. Focusing on your memories with your loved one is essential, not the regrets. However, the power of guilt can make us feel like we never really spent enough quality time with our loved ones, and we missed out on showing our gratitude to them while they were around. Making memories with loved ones is essential, even if they are not physically with you.

The passengers were called to board their flights; all had to wear masks, eye shields, and aprons and started from the boarding point into a bus and finally onto the flight. I had to put a brave face on during this journey, at least until I reached home, and not break down as I travelled through an unfamiliar place. I found my seat, I sat down, and all memories and stories of my dad flashed before me crystal clear. Surprisingly, the next seat to me was empty; I felt my dad's presence and protection all along the journey; after all, he couldn't leave his little daughter alone even when he left his body.

Looking back, sometimes you will never realize how much you can tolerate and face until the situations in your life demand you to do so. I didn't know up to that point that I had that much strength and bravery to face such a challenging situation, keep myself together, and handle the case in the most stable way possible. I also realize today I had a long-term practice of being sound in uncertain situations for years before using meditation, and it came in handy in that critical time of my life. I also learned that having an emotionally healthy life is essential in these times where anything and everything can be uncertain, and the only control one can have is to have self-mastery. Sometimes, I also think that I had blessings from God and all around me that the situation that meant to absolutely break me made me more robust than ever. It happens very often when the pain is so much that it can lead to post-traumatic growth, just like in my case.

The regret I had over that phone call is unexplainable; all my days I spent thinking of making a bright future while sacrificing the present time with my loved ones, just like the saying, "While in search of pearls, I lost the gold in my hand." All these days, I realized how selfish I had been, only thinking about myself, my career, and money while paying less attention to spending time with my loved ones, giving more importance to people's opinions, and ignoring to take action in the present situation and for being so immature. Now, I understand what is essential in life; I am glad I learned it sooner, long before I lost everything. Life is precious; all your loved ones are the most important. Don't fail yourself in taking the best care of them when they are still alive, and you can say I did all I could for my loved ones till their last breath, and I have no regrets.

Sometimes, very challenging situations become the turning point of your life, and it is up to the person facing it to decide whether they will change their life for the good using the lessons learned or to go into depression thinking of all the losses one had. I realize today as I write this book that there is really a choice one has even in the most challenging situation and how important it is for one to be aware of the possibilities of handling the case which will come with working on oneself, understanding oneself, and having a long term practice of seeing possibilities which can happen when one master their emotions, meaning to say while experiencing sorrow, to be aware of the feeling and consciously transform the pain into power. The worst pain in life holds the potential for remarkable transformation, and the sooner one realizes it, the better life becomes for them.

TWO

MEMORY OF A LOVING SON

My superhero, my dad, was born in a city in southern India as the youngest of four children to my grandparents. His father was an accountant, and his mom was a homemaker. Raising four kids was a bit challenging for them due to financial constraints, but the additional responsibility was the health condition of my dad when he was born; he was diagnosed with the congenital syndrome, which involved his heart and required him to have a colostomy bag. I recalled 15 years ago, the chat I had with my grandmom, saying, "Your dad was a sick little baby when he was born, so I protected him and loved him more than the other children." My grandmom had a lot of pride and joy that my dad was her son. She loved to watch him grow and learn new things. She was so excited to see him become a man. He was a small, fragile kid attached to his mom very dearly, and his mom was sure that he would make her very proud in the future. It seemed my dad was always with my grandmom for up to five years as he had a colostomy bag, and my grandmom would put a chair upside down, make my dad sit inside it while she was cooking, and my dad got all attention and love from her. My grandmom had prayed to all gods and every moment wished to the universe that my dad become completely healthy, and all the prayers didn't let her down as my dad gained perfect health after his surgery. My dad was the light of her life, and she was ready to do anything to see my dad blessed with health, wealth, happiness, and prosperity in his life.

As the question queen, even as a small child, I asked my granny, "What made you believe so strongly that my dad would do well despite his condition and your financial status?" My granny told me, "I went to our family ancestral temple and asked about my youngest son's well-being and future; the astrologer said he would definitely do better and go ahead with all you can do. I was not financially supported for the same, so I decided to sell my two gold bangles for 600 rupees for my son's treatment. I took the help of my younger brother and brought him to the hospital, and stayed with him day and night until he completed his two surgeries, one for the heart and one for his colon. Finally, when he was five years old, he was completely well, and I realized my ancestral God hadn't given up on me for every full moon day of a particular month; I made a promise that I would do a pooja to remember all my ancestors and would go to the ancestral temple as a family and show our gratitude which we are following till today."

That story made me look at it the other way: how my grandmom was so determined about her decisions and how lucky my dad was that he got all that extra love and attention from my grandmom. I learned how my grandmom's brave decision and sacrifice in times of uncertainty gave us a chance to experience a great human being, my dad. My grandmom was determined to save and improve my dad's health at any cost. She had to make a lot of sacrifices, but she made it happen. It took a lot of time and energy, but all that mattered to her was to see her son grow more healthily. With the everlasting support of his mom, my dad underwent two major surgeries before the age of five and grew up as a healthy adult. My love and respect for my grandmom is unexplainable; because of her persistence, I had my dad and experienced the wonder of being with such a human. My grandmom looks to me like a living angel who gifted us such a loving dad.

The environment in which my dad grew up was an ordinary middle-class family where my grandfather worked two jobs to earn a livelihood, and my grandmom was a great caretaker who had extraordinary cooking skills and lived in a joint family with brothers of my granddad. As the youngest child, my dad got attention and love from his grandmom and uncles. The eldest uncle of my dad had a huge positive impact on him in cultivating good habits such as cleanliness, honesty, saving money, punctuality, and the importance of being a good-natured, responsible person. My granddad was a very skilled, intelligent person who believed in living in the moment and enjoying life's pleasures. He had excellent organization skills, but a lousy temper masked all his good traits. Sometimes, there were some fights between my grandparents, but what my dad learned out of this surprised me; he grew up precisely as the opposite person in managing his emotions; he was calm and silent and rarely got angry. Maybe he realized how destructive anger can be to people with fragile hearts, just like his mom.

My dad firmly believed that whatever has to happen will happen; if things are meant to happen, no one can stop them or prevent them from happening. One incident he recalled was from his childhood when his grandmom had told him when his dad was a baby, their family had gone to the beach; it had happened that my dad was washed away by the waves, and the same wave returned him to the shore. He said it would not have been prevented if it was my fate. However, I was meant to live; he always said to stop worrying about the things you don't have or feeling bad for something that had happened because what is intended to happen is for everyone's good.

As a son, my dad had immense respect for his parents, never spoke ill of them, and always justified how they cared for him; he would get upset if we would say anything negative about his family members. As a sibling, he was calm, quiet, and playful; he never got into an argument or fight with his brother or sisters. From stories I have heard, they had fun playing together, cracking jokes with loud laughter even as grown-up adults. My dad always has given his family members equal priority, even when he had a family of his own. There was a time when my grandparents needed to look for a different place for themselves due to family issues; my dad beautifully embraced the situation. Even when he lost his job simultaneously, he arranged for my grandparents to live with us on a separate floor. He showed his gratitude to his parents, and as a loving son, it is not a great thing if you have everything. You provided for your parents, but even if one is in a difficult financial situation and still accommodates and chooses to support loved ones not out of compulsion but out of love, that is what makes my dad an extraordinary son.

My dad and granddad had different perspectives on life, food, family, and pretty much everything. Obviously, my dad had some teenage arguments with my granddad, but he never insulted or spoke disrespectfully to my granddad. My dad was a stubborn teenager; if he didn't like to eat crab, he would never eat, irrespective of how many scoldings he needed from my granddad. Though he has expressed how bad he sometimes felt when his dad was judgemental, he always told us it is imperative to respect my grandparents as they have done their best according to their potential.

Since a young age, my dad has very defined likes and dislikes. He doesn't like okra, so no matter how bad someone convinces him to eat it, he will refuse it. He used to jokingly say, "Even if you give me one crore rupees, I won't eat it." He had good cooking skills, especially for making non-vegetarian dishes. Once, my grandmom had a cataract eye operation, and my dad and his brother were cooking for their family members. He loved to cook passionately and made a tasty meal every time. He never reasoned time for not being there for his parents or for not helping them when needed.

You become like the people you surround yourself with. One such influence my dad is from his uncle, my granddad's elder brother, who lived with them; he learned the habit of saving money from a young age. His uncle insisted he put monthly cash in a post office savings account, even if it was a minimal amount, like five rupees. His uncle also emphasized the importance of cleanliness and being neat, so my dad modeled his behavior. As a kid, my dad had an affinity for a quality life; even with old clothes, he made sure they were washed clean, neatly pressed, and looked elegant. He made the best out of whatever he had little access to. Having little was never a reason for him to look shabby or messy.

Another influential person in my dad's life was my grandmom's younger brother, who also motivated my dad to live a meaningful life, make solid investments and save, get a stable job, and even accompany my dad to get a college seat. My dad could identify the right people around him who would help him further in his career and made absolute use of it, and every chance he got, he worked hard and made the fullest out of it. My dad's grandmom was also close to him in terms of pampering and giving unconditional love. Though he had difficulties excelling in academics, he never gave up; he took the help of the positive influences in his life and moved ahead. Being an intrinsically pessimistic person, if I were ever in his position, I would have settled for a lower quality of life, complaining of all my disadvantages. I am glad my dad was different and decided to live a better life and provide a good quality life for his family.

The relationship between my dad and his siblings was pretty good; being the family's youngest child, he was treated as a little brother, and they had fun together playing, laughing, and gossiping. My dad hardly fought with them because of his kind and forgiving nature. I have observed something I felt was unfair towards my dad; my dad accommodated all their mistakes and showed them only love. There were some instances when my dad was pulled into an argument for someone else's mistake; my dad never reacted; he was so calm and let the other person cool and understand the proper perspective. Though it bothered me a lot for my dad to be shouted at for no reason, he didn't like or allow us to talk ill about his siblings anytime.

The siblings of Dad cared for my dad, though their way of expressing it differed. Both my aunts used to express their concern for their brother about his health, long working hours, and his becoming vegetarian; they really did care for him. His elder brother cared for him and always warned my dad to play safe, but my dad risked everything and was unconventional and determined to make our lives way better than his life, and he succeeded in it. When all the elders around him tried to push him to think logically, he went by his heart and showed his family and us that anything is possible.

One peculiar thing my sister shared about my dad is that most of us would first access our resources, opportunities, and capabilities before we set a goal. To put it in plain words, most people would set realistic goals to reduce their disappointment. My dad does precisely the opposite; he would set his goals well before he had the resources or other necessities, work hard toward them, and make them possible. Everyone around my dad felt that he was in some false belief that everything would work out. To all the people who discouraged him, he didn't prove them wrong by his words but with his actions. He always said that people always have something to tell irrespective of what you do; all you need to consider is whether it will do good for you, make you and the people around you better, and work hard for it. Supportive people will come along and help you achieve what you want, but the prerequisite is to make a decision and courageously work towards it even if it seems impossible, and this is a life secret he lived by and taught us.

My dad's elder brother was always protective of my dad. He constantly warned him about the more significant consequences of the recent decisions. He has taught my dad some math, which my dad barely understood. One surprising thing to me was that even as a kid, my dad never compared himself to anyone in the family or the differences in how he treated him. He was always enthusiastic and optimistic, took things lightly, and kept going forward as his only option.

Having God as your friend is one exciting thing my dad used to say to me when he was a kid; he regularly visited the goddess Amman temple near his house, and my dad was religious in paying his visit every Friday; he found immense contentment and happiness going to this particular temple and how he shared all his difficulties to the deity considering her as his friend. Devotion and faith in God are his main anchors in staying strong during times of difficulty, which he imbibed as a small kid.

Having pets, especially dogs, fascinated my dad; he had a German shepherd and Pomeranian before I was born and was very loving and kind to them. Jokingly, he probably trained with them to be a dad first for them before having us. His grandmom loved him, and he got all her love and attention. And they shared a healthy bond as well. Though my dad's circumstances when he was a kid were never that great, be it finance, problems at home, not being so talented or excelling in academics, or his health, he never complained; he always was contented and made the best out of everything. He only appreciated and shared his life's good things and great memories; he would say several people didn't even have what I had.

My dad's kind nature and strong character were partly due to the circumstances in which he had been raised. When he was young, he saw every time my grandfather scolded my grandmom, how she broke down as she was very sensitive. As a child, my dad understood the vulnerable side of people and chose to be kind and not to show the arrogance of being a male to any female whom he came across, be it my mom, us, or his work colleagues. He always respected women and saw potential or only best in all, never used someone's weakness to humiliate them. Also, he saw how his mom had to keep her gold jewels at the pawnshop to feed the family at times; he decided he would never go to the pawn shop ever in his life and followed the same till the end of his life even the most challenging times of his life.

Then comes my dad in the evening from his job, saying, "What are you doing?" I said, "Nothing, simply talking." Then he says, "When I was a student, I used to wake up at 2 AM in the morning and study, and my mom used to wake up and give me a nice tea; I used to work hard those days with the support of my loving mom". My dad told me how important my grandmom was to him, that she was always there for him since he was born and helped him grow into a well-rounded person. He added that my mom is a loving and caring person and has a strong sense of responsibility. She had always told my dad that he needed to be a good person and that it would help him in his life. He took the support of his mom, especially when he was emotionally down, and my grandmom had always been there for my dad, even if it was just to listen to his problems.

My grandmom made my dad feel loved and safe; she was the first person he would say anything to until he had a family. My dad cannot recall when my grandmom didn't love him unconditionally. My grandmom was a great cook, too; she made my dad happy with the tastiest of meals and was nothing but an enthusiastic soul who spread vibrations of joy and protection. In my mind, I was a possessive little daughter "Enough of your mom-son duo!!"

My mom was scolding us for the marks we lost in our exams. Jokingly, my dad said, "You children are getting thrice the mark I used to get; you both will definitely have a brighter future. don't keep crying about the one or two marks you lost." Sometimes, life can be challenging, and falling into the wrong place is easy. It's essential to always stay positive and find the good in every situation. It can be hard to find the good when you are having a bad day, but if you try to find the interest in even the worst situations, you will see that things can turn around. Sometimes, it's just taking a step back and looking at the big picture. My dad is someone who believes that the best is yet to come and that things will get better. He also indirectly made us realize with his joke that it is vital to find the good in a bad situation and to keep working towards betterment. This is one of the easy ways to have a bright life.

People with negative experiences often have the best personalities because they know what it takes to persevere. It takes a lot of courage to face adversity and find happiness in the midst of it; our dad trained us to be optimistic and keep our chin up no matter what happened. What I learned from my superhero was, "One need not be smart and full of talents always to achieve or be someone in life, but definitely one needs to be persistent and hardworking and optimistic so that even the little talent can have great success just like my dad."

Another interesting thing I noticed, a blessing in disguise, is how my dad got that extra love and attention from his mom that made him a person-loving, caring, and respectful person, turning out to be quite different from his other family members. Every sorrow or challenge has a hidden blessing, and by wearing the glasses of optimism, one can see it crystal clear and turn every pain into power. We all have our days where we feel like we are going to burst. We're not as productive as we want to be, we're not as happy as we want to be, and we feel like we'll lose it. It's important to remember that these feelings are blessings in disguise in those moments. It's not that these moments don't hurt; they do. But they are teaching us valuable lessons about who we are and what we are capable of. We should always be thankful for what is happening in our lives and the lessons they teach us.

I also learned, "Don't forget your roots," however mythical it seems, that my grandmom was told by the priest that my dad's sickness was because we forgot to remember and pray to our ancestors. I learned wherever we reach in life, we always look back and be grateful to all those who helped us achieve the dream. We live in a world where we constantly try to reinvent ourselves. We want to be different, unique, and one-of-a-kind. But when we forget our roots and don't appreciate our culture and heritage, we forget what makes us who we are. It's important to celebrate who you are and where you come from. I've never met anyone who doesn't have a story to tell. We all have memories of people and places, but sometimes it takes effort to remember what's important and what's not. Occasionally, we need to recognize the importance of our roots and how much they have helped us in life. If you're ever feeling lost or confused, remember your roots and where you came from. That may help you figure out your life.

THREE

EARLY ADULTHOOD

I remember Dad telling me about his teenage and college days one Sunday morning. My dad said, "In my school days up to 10th standard, everyone in my school mocked me, saying "little elephant" as I used to be a little obese and short. My mom used to cook me great food daily, idli with spicy *kurma*, and I used to eat 12 of them, unlike you children who make such a scene to finish four idlis. Then I used to go to the playground and do hanging exercise every day, and I suddenly grew taller". Looking back as a doctor, I can see it was a constitutional delay of growth, which is a normal phenomenon where, after puberty, adults achieve their maximum height.

I'm not good at taking criticism. I know that when I'm being judged, I need to work on staying focused on what's important and what I need to do to improve. I have many insecurities about my abilities, and I don't like people telling me that I need to work harder or that I am not good enough. So when someone tells me that I am not good enough, I feel a lot of anxiety and stress. But the thing is, criticism can be an excellent motivator for change, just like my dad took his mocking comments about being fat and changed it by exercising and overcoming it rather than being upset about it. After listening to it, I got inspired by the fact that when his peers mocked him, he didn't respond by feeling bad or cursing about it like most of us would do; even at a young age, he always believed that one could change something only by taking some action which he did and eventually overcame that bullying by focusing and working on him rather than picking a fight or being offensive towards his friends and colleagues like most teenagers do.

Dad continued, "Since I was 18, I have started working. I used to wake up at 4 AM in the morning; my mom would pack my lunch; I cycled a few kilometers to reach the train station, go to my workplace, and in the evening, I went to college, he added, "I have been looking after all my expenses since 18 years old". A hardworking and persevering person will put in the time and effort to achieve their goals. This type of person is usually successful in whatever they undertake because they are not afraid of hard work. They understand that success takes time and are willing to put in the position to get there. This is an excellent quality to have in any professional setting.

I asked my dad surprisingly, "What motivated you to do unusual things like waking up so early?" my dad replied, "Your grandfather used to warn me, saying that if I don't perform well, I can only get a job in an industry as a worker something like a person who beats hot steel while manufacturing steel, every time I think about it, it scares me, and I was determined to get a college degree." The power of distant thinking is seeing beyond the immediate problem or situation and thinking about the bigger picture. This can help you find creative solutions to problems and make better decisions. It can also help you better understand the world and how it works. My dad's belief in my granddad's words caused him to make better decisions.

I also asked my dad, "Why has he been self-reliant since a young age?" When he was ten years old, he asked his dad for money for a cinema, but he refused. Once his slippers were torn, his father rudely told him he could not buy him another pair of slippers; at that age, he decided he would never ask anything from his parents. Dignity and self-reliance are two of the most important qualities anyone can possess. Pride usually refers to how we conduct ourselves – whether we show respect and self-worth in our actions and interactions with others. Self-reliance, on the other hand, is more about our internal strength and capability; it's about feeling confident in our abilities and trusting that we can handle whatever life throws our way. Possessing both dignity and self-reliance is a surefire recipe for success in life. Dignified people are usually well-liked and respected by others, while self-reliant people are often seen as strong and capable leaders. My dad chose to be autonomous to keep his dignity and develop great leadership qualities.

On the contrary, when he was a father, he was a totally opposite person, contrary to my grandad. My dad made sure he got every little thing even before we asked for it, and he never said "no" to anything I had ever asked for. He worked hard and provided only the best for us in all aspects of our life. Looking back, he learned how much pain it can cause a kid when he is denied things he wants. He was so protective that we never underwent the same pain that he felt as a young kid. The best type of dad is one who is caring and providing. He is always there for his children, whether they need help with their homework or want to talk about their day. He is a role model and an example of what it means to be a good father. The best type of dad makes his children feel loved and supported, no matter what, and I am proud to say he is one of them.

The insights I got from my father listening to these, my dad was an independent, hardworking, and visionary who believed that great things were possible even when his reality was not so promising. As a dad, it's essential to be both independent and visionary. That means providing for your family and clearly knowing what you want for your future. It can be challenging to balance these two things, but it's essential to try.

Being an independent dad means being able to provide for your family financially. This can be a challenge, but it's crucial to be able to do this for your family's sake. It's also important to be independent in your thinking and decision-making. That means being able to make decisions for your family that are in their best interests, even if they may not be popular. Being a visionary dad means having a clear idea of what you want.

Dad's uncle taught him the importance of saving money right from a young age. Every time my dad got some money, even as little as five rupees, he got a stamp and added it to the post office savings account. Likewise, he saved a few thousand rupees in his early twenties and wanted to buy land. However, the dealer cheated him. My dad didn't have hatred towards that person as the cheater became schizophrenic and committed suicide. He could sue their parents, but my dad didn't, as he felt sympathetic for their loss.

I don't know how my dad's life was before I was born, but I could visualize it from my eldest cousin brother's experiences with my dad on my paternal side. He referred to my dad as "Thaddy mama," which means uncle with a thick and luscious beard, who was his favorite uncle. He loved my dad's mannerism of placing a hand on his chin and looking people straight in his eyes with his head tilted slightly, which he found unique and adopted in his life. My cousin brother, who is a senior manager of a private firm, described to me the event of going to my dad's office, which was a bottle manufacturing unit, and how my dad gave him a tour of the plant; everyone wished my dad since he was tiny at that age, he presumed that my dad was the owner of the company, and I burst into a burst of vast laughter hearing that. My dad had taken his sister and my cousin brother to the beach, where they enjoyed the peanuts, played, and made it a memorable evening. This also reminds me of my dad's experience with his first nephew, who passed away at a younger age; he said how the baby would smile brightly on seeing him, how they played together, and how he felt his heart broken about his nephew passing away.

Our grandmom had undergone cataract surgery in both eyes when my dad was in his early twenties before his marriage. My dad and brother had cooked for the family for the entire month, along with caring for my grandmom. It made me realize how much love and care they had for their family and their responsible nature. The location where they lived at this time had a problem with the water supply, and my dad and his siblings would be awakened early in the morning at three a.m. to fetch water for the family. My dad had sometimes felt annoyed, but he used to mock us, saying that I should have woken up you children as I did, and then you would stop complaining of the little discomforts around you.

As a young adult, he had specific likes and dislikes. This reminds me of an incident when all my dad's family members were at the dining table, ready to have their dinner. My dad dislikes crab, and my granddad, an authoritative father, insisted he eat the crab. Even after a lot of advice and argument, my dad never touched it. As a young man, he was very decisive; once he held on to something, he never let go of that interest or dislike for things around him. But this attitude was totally opposite when it came to dealing with people; even if someone was rude or behaved unreasonably with him, he was always kind, forgiving everyone, and never hurting anyone.

Working for experience instead of salary can be a great way to gain the skills and knowledge you need to further your career. While you may be paid less than you would like, you can earn a lot of valuable experience that will help you in the long run. Working for expertise can help you network and build connections in your chosen field. My dad worked part-time for meager pay for about two years. Because of his hard work and persistence, he got placed in a company as an assistant manager after completing his bachelor's degree in commerce. Shortly after, his parents started to have a marriage conversation.

In many cultures, it is customary for parents to initiate marriage talks with their children. This is often done when the children are of marrying age, which can vary depending on the culture. These talks aim to discuss the expectations and responsibilities of marriage and help the children decide whether or not they want to get married. In some cases, the parents may also talk to the prospective spouse's parents to get to know them better and ensure they are compatible with their children. These talks can be constructive in ensuring that both parties are on the same page about the marriage and can help avoid misunderstandings or problems.

In India, marriage is more of a responsibility of the parents rather than the individuals getting married. This is because arranged marriages are more common in India, and the parents have to take care of finding a suitable match for their child. Once a compatible partner is found, the parents must take care of the wedding arrangements and ensure everything goes smoothly. Finding a bride can be long and complicated, especially if you need help figuring out where to start. There are a few different ways to find a potential bride, and weighing your options before deciding is essential. One option is to go through a matchmaker, who can help you find a suitable bride based on your specific preferences. Finally, you could also find a bride through more traditional means, such as attending social events or being introduced to potential brides by friends and family members. Whichever route you decide to take, it's essential to be patient.

My dad's uncle had a friend looking for a bridegroom for his niece. That eventually led both families of my mom and dad to make further arrangements for marriage. Both parties had expectations of having a good character person with a college degree and from the same caste. The families were quite comfortable with each other, and now it was time for my mom and dad to approve marriage.

The bridegroom is a fit, slim, handsome young man with glasses. He is an excellent choice for any bride who wants an attractive groom and a person of character. At this point, my parents had not met each other, but their families had met each other. My mom was not very much convinced at first sight, yet on suggestions of her mom and dad that my dad was a person of character and that my mom's dad liked him, my mom agreed to marry him. There began an adventurous journey for my dad, having a new family member who was about to change his life drastically for the good.

FOUR

A LOVING FATHER

One fine Sunday, my dad went to meet my mom in her home; my mom said, "When your dad came to meet me, he had many grey hairs, and that she told her mom the same. Your dad didn't even bother to dye his hair while coming to see the bride". I thought to myself, "What a transparent, honest person with integrity my dad was; I felt so surprised about his honesty ."My dad instantly liked my mom, as he always said that my mom was very beautiful, and he instantly agreed to marry her.

The engagement was done in a simple manner. My dad was blessed to have a good, intelligent bride and great in-laws. My mom's dad was such a lovely person; he loved my dad like his own son; their relationship was so thick that when my granddad passed away, my dad wrote a three-page poem for his father-in-law as he was in immense sorrow and needed to let it out in some way. The respect, love, care, and attention that my dad received from my mom's family made him feel blessed to have chosen my mom to be his wife. My dad never demanded any jewels or dowry from my mom's family and was ready to accept even if they sent only my mom to his house.

The marriage happened smoothly in our hometown with the blessings of all the family members. Initially, my mom struggled to adjust to the family as she was introverted, and my dad was in a joint family. My dad had a very accepting and non-judgemental approach toward my mom; he accepted her wholeheartedly and trusted her. Trust is the main foundation of any beautiful relationship. Their beautiful life started on the foundation of trust, transparency, and belief in each other. My mom slowly adapted to my dad's family during the first year of marriage. She was pregnant with my sister. My dad listened to my mom patiently, especially when my mom didn't like some behavior of my dad. My dad always said my mom was his greatest gift, companion, guide, and turning point in his life. My dad had immense respect for my mom; he never got angry at my mom and showed us how a woman should be treated.

I always admired, wondered at, and witnessed the most beautiful relationship between my mom and dad. My dad was humble yet assertive, always respected, and never shouted or insulted my mom or made her feel small. He considered mom the most important person in the family, and he listened and acknowledged her wise decisions, implemented them, and gave my mom sole responsibility of managing the family's finances. He never showed the ego of earning money or his position as a manager. At home, he always took the role of a loving husband and a happy father. My mom was also a perfect counterpart to my dad; she never spoke ill of my dad to others, always showed respect, and had total honesty, transparency, and trust between them. The couple was truly meant to be, and destiny designed this beautiful relationship to flow with harmony each day. It was a treat for us to watch; I was under the illusion that all families were happy and harmonious up to a certain age.

To keep the harmony of the family, both my dad and mom made many sacrifices, like changing of food preferences of my mom by cooking the vegetables my dad liked, never doing things that could irritate my dad not out of fear but out of love for him, waiting for my dad till he arrives to have family dinner together, my dad being tolerant to short tempered nature of my mom at times understanding the logic and justification behind her anger, saying sorry even when he is not wrong, or giving preference to my mom's decision of how and where the family would spend their weekends.

As I grew up, I understood any beautiful relationship requires a lot of sacrifice, understanding, and standing together by each other's side even when the odds are against you, and I set it as my model for my relationships.

Soon, marriage was over, and a year later, my elder sister was born. My dad had taken my cousin brother to visit my elder sister when she was just delivered to show his pride and joy as a dad. A good husband now was promoted to being a dad. The dad side of him was the best decoration or attribute of his character.Every day, he came home excited to see his little angel grow and glow beautifully from the inside out. My dad wished and promised himself that he would only give the best life to his little angel.

He told my mom "We will have only one kid and provide her the best life". However my grand mom on both sides said "No, no as the baby grows up, she needs a companion to play with and a relation in future, so it is ok to have a second kid". That's how I came into my parents' life. All these discussions had happened once they realised when my mom conceived for the second time six months after her dad's death. Though my mom had not come out of her dad's passing away, I was a good reason for her to take care of herself in a better way and look up for better things coming her way. My dad always loved kids very much he liked to play with them, feed, and dress them up, and was excited for the arrival of the second kid.

I could recall one incident my mom had told me: my dad was an occasional drinker; after my sister was born, one day, my dad came home after a party, continuously gargling his mouth. My mom told him, "Dear Viji, see, now we have a child, and you have a private job; it's not like you have a government job where you will get a pension if something happens to you; all these habits are not good for your health, and it will have an impact on our daughter in future, think about it and make a decision. That night, my dad gave up his habit of drinking forever. I could hardly believe it when we grew up and heard this story, but it was the truth.

Three years after my sister was born, I was the second daughter. Living in India and coming from a traditional family, many people in the family felt and discussed that he should have got a son, having no idea how he is about to raise his two daughters more like a son and make the world wonder if it was even possible to raise daughters like this and the most famous quote in his funeral will be "Glad, he has brought up his two daughters so well, independent, educated, bold and self-reliant, and how he has raised us like boys with freedom and autonomy what a good job he did as a great father," given the fact that we both are not married at this point. Irrespective of the world's views, opinions, and judgments, my dad was absolutely delighted to have me in his life, and there began one of the most incredible, loving, and beautiful relationships between my dad and me.

When I was about six months old, my grandparents kept my mom and dad in a separate house a year after the death of my maternal grandfather. My mom hadn't come out of the pain, and the young couple had to manage a home independently. This was a challenging phase of their life as they needed to manage their finances, put a kid in school and a baby at hand, and my mom was not that great at cooking or doing household chores. My parents also recalled this time as the one that gave them the freedom to make bold choices and the start of their growth as a family. Once I was ill, my mom had to take me to the nearby primary healthcare center to get medicines for me after paying five rupees as a token fee. My dad worked hard all his life, made my mom the house queen, and was ready to keep anything at stake for our great future. He never overthought anything; he was simple carefree, always focusing on what was needed and how it could be done. He never worried or complained and showed us how to make the impossible possible.

A famous phrase all would have heard is, "I was brought up in the streets." When I was around three years old, I was loved by everyone in my street; I always played in the street with other kids, visited each house in the street every day, and was dear to all, maybe because I was a cute little mischievous kid and entertained everyone. After bathing and having breakfast, I went roaming to the house owner's home downstairs, a single Brahmin lady, followed by the neighborhood houses to play with other kids. One such day, I was playing with two boys, and accidentally, my finger got stuck in the grill gate, and I screamed and cried, the whole street gathered there. My mom took me to the naturopathy doctor near my home. On getting me treated, my mom was curious about the little red light at the corner of the room named Shivbaba. She asked the doctor, and she was invited to learn meditation. My mom and dad went and learned meditation, which significantly shaped their character, skills, and life. We went along with our parents and learned meditation at the very young age of seven years. This raja yoga meditation made me and my family more resilient, calm, peaceful, and happy. My dad, a vegetarian, became vegetarian, meditated daily, attended all Sunday classes, and followed all disciplines. My parents made this courageous, wise decision at such a young age, which proved beneficial in their later stages. All the struggles that came their way caused them discomfort. Still, because they mastered their emotions using meditation, they didn't project their suffering anytime to us. They could think clearly and straight in the most demanding and chaotic situations. My dad insisted on us attending meditation classes, becoming vegetarian, and following the principles of not getting angry, greedy, or self-centered. Later in my life, all these skills came in handy for me to resolve all the conflicts I faced from the world around me.

While my parents became vegetarian, my sister and I were allowed to eat non-vegetarian at my grandparents' or uncle's house; however, my dad and I would argue about it. Though I was very young, around seven years old, I spoke a lot; my dad told me, "Dear Vinu, eating non-vegetarian is not good." I said, "Listen, Daddy, when you were a kid, you ate meat, and when you became older, you became vegetarian; likewise when I am grown up, I will do the same." Looking back, I can see how gentle and respectful my dad was. However, when I was a kid, he treated me like an equal, listened to what I had to say, left the decisions to my choice, and was not forceful. My dad's parenting skill is unique in making us clearly understand why we do what we want to do as a prerequisite before acting it out. Sometimes, parents can be great teachers, and he was one of them

I grew up seeing my dad having a disciplined routine like meditation, healthy food, punctuality, and sincerity at his workplace and spending quality time with us at the end of the day. He followed his routine and never compromised his habits, even if the situations were unfavorable. One thing I admire about my dad and am still trying to imbibe is being religious in my routine. I have seen my dad; if he decides on something, he puts in a hundred percent hard work every day and never gives excuses. Once, he gave me a schedule for preparing for my postgraduate entrance exam, and it was so difficult that I never followed it. But my dad used that schedule to study as a kid. I still admire that and hope someday that gene of him in me gets activated, and I change for the good.

Having your parent as your friend is something incredible. Our dad played with us at our level. Once, my sister was a very small kid, she had asked what my dad was eating, and he mockingly opened his mouth to show the chocolate to tease her; my sister, being a smart kid, had taken that chocolate and swallowed it, till today he will tease my sister with this incident. He was never a strict, distant, or unapproachable dad but a very loving, cheerful, and playful one.

We always felt that we were the most precious among everything he had in his life. I remember the days when I was in Kindergarten how my dad used to lift me from the bed, bring me to the washroom, take a brush with paste and keep it in my mouth, bathe me, dress me up, comb my hair, put powder and bindi, how he used to stuff the idli in my mouth and bring me out to the road and put me in the van, all in half an hour. Looking back, I can see how lazy and uncooperative I was and how my dad was patient, loving, and caring.

Anyone can give birth to a child, but parenting the child the right way is an art that only a few people have mastered. One essential requisite of a great parent is patience and tolerance; when I was a baby, I used to be adamant and cry aloud for anything and everything. My dad always picked me up, consoled me, and never got angry, saying that I was a small kid and didn't understand right and wrong. He instantly comforted me every time with his love and understanding and listened to me patiently all the time. Everyone around me thought that he was spoiling me, but he was teaching me an art that I use with my nieces and nephews. I got a lot of comments when I was a kid for being chubby, like "Where does your mom get rice for you?" my dad always accepted and appreciated me for who I was and encouraged me to eat healthy and stay happy and never mind the people around me. In the later part of my life, I realized that you teach children not by advising them but by being a role model, and even minor incidents can profoundly impact your child's mind.

My dad played with me every day. I used to look forward to the horn sound of his bike rushing to the gate with a big smile to receive him. We ate our dinner together; he used to get the snacks for us. On Sundays, he cooked us dishes like bisibelebhath, rice, rasam, and potato fry. He used to take us to the meditation class with him. He encouraged us to communicate with the sisters there. Somehow, today, I have the ease of talking to any unknown person boldly because my dad trained me unconsciously. Unknowingly, he also taught us the importance of having good company and living life with values.

Once I remember, my dad got me, my elder sister, and my cousin sister a small rainbow-colored umbrella and colored hangers for us. It was the gift I received from my dad when I was very young, and I was jumping with joy. I remember even today how much happiness I felt. I grew up soon; it was time for me to go to school, and my parents took me for admission to the same school my elder sister studied. My dad used to mock me, saying how I was wearing a red t-shirt and blue jeans, and never opened my mouth for any question asked by the headmistress, but in the end, I just got the chocolate and came home.

As we grew up, we did well in our academics and participated in extracurricular activities such as oration, chess, badminton, basketball, karate, and uniformed services like scouts and guides. We brought home several certificates, and our dad was so happy to see us win and flourish in our school. He was proud of us, always made us feel that we were doing a great job, and never compared us with anyone.

I was very attached to my dad; I felt the feeling of owing him. I would get agitated if anyone even teased me, saying, "Your dad is my uncle first; you were born after that, so he was our uncle before he became your dad." I would frown at them, hold my dad's hand, and would walk away angrily when I was a kid. I admired him as I felt that he was an ideal person whom I needed to look up to; every relative had only good things to say about my dad, like how calm he was, just opposite to me, who cried and was adamant about every little thing, how a gem of a person he was, I grew up hearing these words. I also knew that even if the whole world disagreed with what I perceived as correct, I would always have my dad support me. He was also an excellent healer; once I came back after writing a scholarship exam, I ran into our home hurriedly to see my aunt, who had got chocolates for us. I just slipped on the granite floor, hit my head against the bedroom door, and got a cut in my eyebrow with profuse bleeding. I was crying my lungs out; my dad picked me up, consoled me, and did the first aid. Since he was a reiki practitioner, he made me lie down and gave me a healing session of thirty minutes of reiki. I healed the wound without any sutures; every time I look in the mirror, the beautifully healed eyebrow reminds me of my wonderful dad.

Walking the talk is the most challenging thing to do. Still, my dad showed us how to have a balanced life between materialism and inner stability. He showed us the power of meditation, being disciplined, and working towards a life with comfort yet being humble and frugal in the present. He always made us believe anything is possible and never discouraged us from exploring the new. Yearly, once, my mom and dad go on a meditation retreat to Rajasthan for a week or ten days. Since our school was strict on giving us leave, they took turns going for the retreat. On the days my mom was far from our home, our dad took care of us with such deep love and care, right from waking us up, sending us to school, to cooking to making us go to bed, along with his office work. It was such a unique experience to have our dad taking up the role of our mom as well.

A few years later, his company got shut down, and my dad had to look for a new job, trying a couple of businesses in between. But throughout this challenging financial situation, we had no clue what was happening because we were provided with more than what he could afford. He sent us to one of the best private schools in my hometown in a private van, admitted both of us to karate classes, got us everything, and most important of all, both my mom and dad never mentioned a word about lack of money, we got to hear all these only as tales when we stepped into our college.

I recall my mom saying to my dad, "If we need to be shifted to another school with lesser fees," my dad gave an iconic reply, "Whether we save loads of money or asset to our children, we don't know now; however I want to give them the best education possible for that would be their real asset in their life, though they are girls, I want them to be independent and not at the mercy of their partners."

If someone could say these words when in a good situation, that is comprehensible, but being in a financially challenging situation, my dad had said, that too being very firm on it makes me wonder how different his thought process was and how much of a visionary he was and above all the kind of love he had for us, every time I think of this, I see him only as a superhero.

During this crisis, he tried several other businesses, gave many interviews, and successfully landed in a manager position again. I remember he used to start from our home at seven- thirty in the morning, get his office bus, travel around two hours to reach his office and come home by seven thirty in the evening. When he came home, he never complained about his day or job, refreshed himself and called us for dinner, played with us, and cherished us dearly, even at the end of the tiring day. My dad never sacrificed his quality time with us; though he could have tried for jobs away from our hometown, he persisted even if it took him some time to get a job so that we wouldn't miss him or his sustenance. Looking back, our dad gave us more non-physical treasures such as his quality time, education, attention to our acts, cooking for us, being there for us emotionally, and protecting us from any bad company. There is no doubt we got the best of the physical things as well, such as fancy dresses, tasty meals, and pastries, but our happiness and the reason for which we remember him today is because of his unconditional love, which no money can replace.

My dad's struggles during his employment were walking three kilometers to save money and getting a bus from there to reach our home. We never knew that all the struggles were happening because my mom and dad never showed us any pain of theirs and made sure we had everything. Our family had a sound support system; my uncle rented their house to us at a low price, my grandmom and aunt funded some provisions, and my uncle paid for our van fees. Looking back, I am still astonished at how they managed to raise us with more than what they were capable of at that moment and never showed a small sign of discontentment that we had no clue until years later when we had fully grown up. Such love of my parents makes me feel overwhelming gratitude every single day. I couldn't have had it any better, and I realize that the greatest treasure I have is their unconditional, selfless love.

Years later, when all of the financial constraints settled, when I was in higher secondary school, I was very stressed from long hours, no time for extracurricular activities, and travel from my home, but I never complained. But my dad was so observant and started to drop me at school every morning. Though he had a tightly packed schedule, he chose to make me a priority. He willingly took additional discomfort to show his love and care with little but meaningful endeavors. Many things for which we remember our dad are not for some grand events but for the little things he did and the way he made us feel so loved and privileged.

When my dad got an illness, he never bothered; he took his medicines and followed the doctor's advice but was carefree mentally; he always affirmed that he was as strong as steel and behaved in the same way too. But when we got ill or hurt, he would absolutely lose it all. Once, my sister got a cut in her leg as the bench fell on her feet in school. When my mom called my dad to come home earlier to visit the doctor, he became so worried and rushed back home. I understood how attached our dad was to us.

There were many days when I argued with my dad; even as a very small kid, he never discounted me or ignored my silly questions; he answered all patiently. I have asked my dad, "How does it matter that I need to be good to others when the world doesn't seem to run on idealistic principles?" my dad said, "Even if the whole world is doing wrong, it is never your responsibility, but every action you take becomes your habit and determines your future. You also can never blame the other person for your action, saying they did this, so I reacted like this; still, you will be held accountable for your responses. Even if the world continues the same, you cannot lower your integrity because of the situation or another person; most of all, God is watching you silently so that you will be rewarded for your good actions in one way or another. When most people are in a reaction mode, just mirroring the other person's action, you also have an opportunity to respond. People will mirror your action and will have a ripple effect, and the world will be a better place because you were in it if you lived the right way."

Every time I got into a conflict with my dad, the way he handled it was absolute magic; at the end of the conversation, he always made me feel how much he loved me. It was so massive that my anger would dissolve in front of his heart-warming behavior. The days I disagreed with my dad are very few, and I remember them crystal clear. Once, I was watching television in my grandmom's house in the adjacent flat. My dad told me to go to sleep so that it would be easy for me to wake up in the morning; as I didn't listen to him, he got angry and said, "Are you coming now, or I will lock the door," I just couldn't speak a word in front of him and with tears in my eyes and ego hurt, I went to sleep angrily. The following day, my dad only came and spoke to me. I was so upset that I ignored him, but with his overwhelming love and tactics, I lost it and just forgot everything and played with him.

My family only goes out on long trips occasionally; the ones I remember today are visiting a retreat center near the city's border yearly and going to the retreat center a few thousand kilometers away from my hometown. We were exposed to being part of a community that is free from differences of religion, region, and ethnicity, and living by morals was instilled at a very young age. We went to visit museums, temples, parks, and meditation halls up in the hilly area. Our dad always had an eye on what we were doing, showed and explained the unique things that we didn't know before, and was very protective. We had tasty snacks together and walked, talking about the amusement of the new things we had learned on the way.

Once, I was in my early teens; I was very adamant, and a fight broke out between my mom and me. My mom complained to my school teacher about my behavior; it was very much bothering me as it disrupted my ego and my reputation in school. I felt so bad that I said I wouldn't go to that school anymore and was very firm on that. My dad called me and explained to me why I was wrong and why my coping mechanism for the problem was wrong as well. He taught me irrespective of whether things are in your favor or not; you need to have the courage to face the world. It doesn't matter what people think of you; what is more important is what you feel about yourself. Making a mistake is not wrong, but not learning from it is definitely not good. My dad had a loving, smart, and logical way of getting me back on track, and he is one of the very few persons who could face me and convince me in conflicting situations. I am very argumentative and have an unforgiving attitude, especially when I am really angry. I slowly learned it is a skill; he was an excellent conflict resolver, which he practiced over the years, and I imbibed from him eventually.

Shortly after I returned from abroad and took my licensure exam, I told my dad I wanted to do an online business after reading a book about it. I was fascinated by the idea, but my dad gave me a straight "no" in this matter. At times, my dad seemed overprotective of me, especially in adventurous, unknown areas of life. I did feel at times that my dad had limiting beliefs about the unknown things and ignored them even without exploring them, but now I understand that it was all because that was his way of protecting us.

Soon, I went to the northern part of India to pursue my coaching classes for the licensure exam. I decided to stay outside the hostel in an unknown place. My dad was never skeptical; he spoke to his boss; they had an office there, so he let me stay there for six months by myself. He had immense trust and faith in us, believing that we would make it somehow. My mom was very much against this idea, but my dad convinced my mom and helped me experience this adventure. Because he allowed me to do it, I later went to other southern states of India. I lived by myself and could handle anything that came my way like it was nothing.

After I became a doctor, I asked my dad to get me a two-wheeler for going for my internship. It is the only thing my dad refused even after continuously nagging him for a long time. He told me, "Even if you stand upside down, you will never get a bike; I don't want you to get hurt or involved in some accidents in this city of traffic; rather, you can take a cab every day." It was initially unacceptable for me; I always thought my dad believed we should be independent and bold, but now he scares me of such a small thing. But he was very firm; instead, he dropped me off at the hospital every morning. He had such a balance of being loving yet strict in some aspects. He disciplined me in the sweetest way possible whenever I got off track.

My last conflict with my dad was fifteen days before he passed away. I was working in a remote location away from home. I had come home due to the second wave of COVID-19; for some reason, I never wanted to return. I told my parents I felt I was missing home and would join a covid duty here. My dad got so upset because the tickets were booked. I informed the management that I would be there and then decided not to go; for some reason, an undeniable feeling in my heart of longing told me clearly to stay back, and I voiced my opinion, too. My dad told me, "Listen, Vinusha, you have put your postgraduation entrance exam center there; last-minute travel may be unpredictable, so if you finish your exam the same night, I will book a return flight ticket for you."

Moreover, his reason was that I am a professional and should behave accordingly, maintain integrity, keep my word, and be a reliable person to the management. When I told him I didn't want to go, I remember vividly him sitting on the sliding chair, very upset and frowning. I didn't particularly appreciate seeing my dad that way to be upset because of me, so I said I would go.

Looking back, it was the universe's way of telling me to spend the precious quality time left with him, but I succumbed to logic and pleasing my other family members and decided to go to my workplace without having a single clue that morning was the last day I would see him in person alive. I also thought the other way: if I were ever around him, I would not have let him quickly go; maybe he knew well in advance that he couldn't deny the request of his loving daughter to stay back or that I would have gone crazy and into complete emotional shock and would have taken a long time to recover if I had to witness my dad leaving us forever. Sometimes, I also think it was God's way of protecting me from the increased suffering because I was far away and alone; I had time to process my emotions before I saw him lifeless in front of my eyes. I had to stay composed because I was with people who knew me only officially and not personally; it gave me a chance to respond to the crisis rather than reacting and losing it all.

The last few conversations I had with my dad reminded me of some advice he gave me. It was my mom's birthday, and I had ordered some gifts for her. My dad was happy that I cared about Mom, but he told me, "Dear, you should stop spending too much; just because you have money in hand doesn't mean that you spend as you wish; your intention of doing good is always appreciated, but you need to be wise in how you spend your money, start the habit of saving, even if it is pennies, one day it will become a significant amount. During the first wave of COVID-19, my sister was in another state. She had asked my dad if she had to return as she was working from home, but the ticket was costly, and she had second thoughts about her travel during COVID-19. My dad, without any doubt, said to her, Whatever it costs, it's okay; you come back, we will take care. Had she not come that day, exactly one day later, inter-state travel restrictions were imposed, and she would have been locked in that city for six months. I always felt my dad had a strong sense of right and wrong, and he had it all well defined in his head well ahead of time. He repeatedly told us to see if it is necessary, then you can even spend one crore rupees on it, but if it is not necessary, don't buy it even if it is only one rupee. He lived by the same principle; he was ready to make me join an internship in a government college, which was expensive, but refused to buy me a bike, which cost way less than that. I knew even if I followed this one thing; I would have a financial fortune at the end of my life

FIVE

A LOYAL MANAGER

When my Dad was around 30, he faced two of life's biggest challenges. One, the company he worked in for 12 years shut down; second, he was diagnosed with a cardiac condition. This was one crucial time of his life when his decisions could make him sink or swim. My Dad faced them courageously; he suffered, but it was never visible on his face or activities. He was enthusiastic, always looking for betterment opportunities with a spirit of never giving up. Most importantly, he saw and utilized the good side of it; he got more time with us, made the most of it, and made an everlasting loving bond with us emotionally.

In his entire life, my Dad worked only for two companies, both his bosses being North Indians, who symbolized Vijayakumar as a figure of loyalty and trustworthiness. Under the worst circumstances, he never left his boss's side; one time, when I heard the first company he was working for, due to debt issues, my Dad and his boss were locked overnight from outside by the creditors and threatened, my Dad still didn't leave the company until his boss said we couldn't run the office anymore.

Apart from being a great dad, he was also an excellent manager. He was very responsible for any work his boss gave him; he finished it however challenging or impossible it may seem without giving excuses. He was brave when he had to put complex, conflicting thoughts across the table to his boss without fearing the consequences, and he always believed and expected his employees to do one hundred percent in their jobs to be punctual and loyal. Even during his holidays, he always picked up office calls and settled matters that needed immediate attention beyond what his job description called for.

I remember conversing with his second boss, whom he joined two years after losing his first job, saying, "Vijayakumar is one of my close friends and extended family; he is very hardworking and trustworthy." I feel Dad sacrificed his entire life for work, working almost 10 hours each day, six days a week, with the idea of providing only the best for us; he saw his job as the way of freedom to our lives. He had very tough times like the employee resignation, strike for a pay rise, extended travel to sign documents, and going to court hearings; despite his work environment, not even a single day did he come home and complain about his job neither did he displace his anger on us, such a golden soul he was.

Be the best in what you do, and the rest will follow. We all have heard this: when my Dad joined the second company, he was the administrative officer; he gained the trust of his boss, managed the house construction of the boss's house, and slowly progressed to managing the real estate project of his boss as deputy general manager. It doesn't matter if you hold an insignificant position at the beginning of your career, but you fail when you don't become a significant part of the company when you retire. I saw a post from the employee of the company in which my Dad worked saying that my Dad's place is still empty and no one can ever replace him as the quality and the level of dedication he had to his work was more than one could ever imagine.

I got to hear from my Dad sometimes about his workplace. When he initially needed to improve in English, he started with just yes or no, slowly talking in one or two sentences to finally speaking fluently. He never refrained from taking an opportunity because of a lack of skills but used it to grow or get better at the same skill. Once, there was a fight between two workers, and my Dad sat to resolve the issue; he told us sometimes, even when you understand that the employee has clearly done wrong when you are a decision-making authority, you need to take into account the long term consequences of a decision, he also shared how he settled the matter within the institution rather than taking it legally as it would have made those two workers unemployed for a lifetime. Being empathetic when you are in a place of power can do magic; people will be obsessed with having this kind of leader, and I would proudly say my Dad was one of them.

One day, when my Dad and I came back after I had written my Hindi exam, we saw the old union leader of his first company, who met my Dad almost after ten years saying to me, "Sir is such a great person, whatever conflict we had at workplace, he just did his job taking the side of the management, outside which he is such a humble, kind and empathetic person and no one can ever be like him, having the balance of being a great manager without compromising his values as a human being." I was thinking to myself."
I never knew Dad handled conflicts at his workplace with such grace and dignity; I was surprised how he keeps all the good things he has done for himself that I have to hear it from a third party every time.

Once, the builder of our home went to my Dad's office, returned, and told my mom, "At the office, Sir is busy and handles multiple issues simultaneously; I wonder how calm he is despite all his circumstances. Whenever I see Sir at home, he is so calm and smiling; I wonder how he manages all the stressors so effortlessly, and my Dad, though in a place of power, doesn't show off when he is at home". When I heard this, I knew that's why my Dad is a superhero.

Whenever my Dad comes across conflicts at his workplace, he gracefully handles them; he politely writes to his boss as to how his perspective is not correct, never gets into a heated argument about who is right, instead keeps calm at times of crisis and will open up later, this is one of his secrets of keeping his job for a very long time. When other jealous employees badmouthed my Dad, he gained such a reputation from his boss that his boss would call him and inform him about these misunderstandings without giving an ounce of belief to the gossipers. My Dad was not always calm at the workplace; if he felt something was wrong, he confronted them authoritatively and made them realize their flaws to give a more productive output.

I had a glimpse of my Dad's nature of work when I had a chance to observe him during COVID-19 when he had worked from home. The finance was a primary concern for all, so the salary of people was reduced and delayed. My Dad was very proactive in ensuring the salary went to the employees on time despite the difficulties; he was a humanitarian; he put himself in other people's shoes and urged the matter as if it were his salary. Similarly, my Dad tried to convince his boss to pay earlier for bonuses during occasions such as Diwali so that those families have time to purchase peacefully. When in a position, one tends to focus on one's work and difficulties rather than being a people server. I am proud of my Dad for being a humanitarian before he played the managerial role.

During the COVID-19 time, rules, regulations, and restrictions kept changing now and then when the government released their orders. My Dad was an avid reader; he read the notification as soon as it was released from start to end and made quick decisions for the office. I never knew my Dad was that smart in understanding something and adapting it so quickly. He had a continuous learning policy; he attended Zoom calls with other managers in the state and imbibed the guidelines in his own office. I saw that proactive leader part of him during this period of which I had no clue before. I have seen him read his spiritual study every morning religiously with a pen so seriously that I understood how vital everyday learning was to stay on top of your game in any role one plays.

I remember talking to his boss two days after my Dad passed away; I told him that even for us, I don't have a single complaint that he didn't do anything for us; he has done more than enough for us, good enough to lead a settled life for both of us, though he passed away suddenly, I am delighted with his role as a dad for us.

However, we miss him for his presence and regret that I couldn't do all the things I wished to do for him to show my gratitude to him. His boss said that he resonated with the same, that in the project my Dad was handling, only three or fewer flats remained for sale, and he had finished all his work in his office. It was a significant loss for the company, almost equal to us, as he was more than an employee.

As a manager, my Dad displayed tremendous empathy for all who worked with him. Amidst his busy work and calls, he noticed that his office boy brought only rice and very little plain curry; he asked him why he wouldn't get a proper lunch every day. The office boy replied that his wife didn't know how to cook, and due to some financial issues, my Dad shared his meal every day with him and used to tell my mom how much the office boy enjoyed the tasty meal she had prepared. When someone reaches a position, they tend to overlook their subordinates' difficulties, but my superhero was different, very observant, and considerate of everyone around him.

Part of my Dad's job was to hire and train new people for his office. He was so good at choosing the right person; maybe it comes with experience, and he trained them like his children. The world today can be a tough place for freshers or juniors in any company, but my Dad connected with them emotionally first, made them part of the family, made them feel at ease, and groomed them in their skills; he was so good that years after they left the company they still remembered my Dad's teachings and stayed in contact and even came for his funeral.

Very recently, after my Dad's first death anniversary, I met my Dad's colleague and a friend who described how humble my Dad was; he was the signing authority of the real estate project. when everyone used to wait at the registry office for the concerned person to come to sign and hand over the project, my Dad used to go on a bike, his mannerisms being very humble and down to earth to the point where people asked: "Why doesn't sir at least come in a car?" I was thinking to myself, "That's because he invested and valued his daughter's future more than his comfort; even when there are times

I would pester my dad to buy a car, he will discount the idea by distracting me with another topic saying "It's not a necessity."

In this world of show business, I learned from my Dad how authentic he was, economical, and invested only in things that he thought were essential, irrespective of what people around him said or did.

SIX

A VISIONARY OF THE FUTURE

Years ago, my mom shared a conversation that she had with Dad while I was in her womb, "We used to watch a television show in which a businessman has two daughters suddenly pass away, and his daughters take over the business and show leadership like men, your dad said, "It would be good if the second child is a girl and they both are bold, independent, smart and self-reliant like the characters shown on the television, wouldn't that be great ?" My mom smiled and said, "Yeah, it would be nice if that happened."

At every stage of our lives, despite the existing financial difficulties, Dad never let us think small. He always talked about abundance and how my sister and I would be well-educated and successful in all aspects of life. His famous line was, "Education is the biggest asset." Since my sister and I performed pretty well in school, he was even more reassured that we would fulfill his dreams.

My dad used to tell us how he wanted to build us a twin house on his land later when I became a doctor, he dreamt of building a hospital, and he used to jokingly say, "When Vinu starts earning, she will earn so abundantly that she will just put hands in her pocket and pull out all the money and give it to the family," he envisioned that I would be so successful. Listening to all this, I used to ask myself, 'Why is my dad even in dreamland? See, I am not even earning a good amount, and he is thinking of abundance,' and I used to doubt my ability, seeing him being so optimistic and having immense faith in me.

My dad believed, "My children should be one step ahead of me in all aspects of life." Before I joined medicine, I took a Bachelor of Science course in Psychology; my dad was so upset and felt let down that "If I have done a Bachelor of Commerce, and your sister is a Bachelor of Technology, how can you take an ordinary course similar to mine." He made arrangements and sent me abroad to study medicine. My dad was very intolerant of small ideas, things with less quality, disrespectful behavior, and always envisioned something that we could not even think of way before it all manifested.

My dad taught me a beautiful lesson at a young age: "If one family has to move to the next level or class in terms of standard of living, then one person in their entire generation would have struggled so hard to bring about that change." Instead of saving money for himself or making us live a mediocre life, he was precisely the kind of person who put all his energy and effort into making us go to the next level with financial freedom so that entire generations would benefit from it. He firmly believed that it was possible even before the situation favored him.

Once I asked my dad how my elder sister's marriage had to be conducted, he said his vision was that he would have to invite a minimum of one thousand people of his contacts who constantly ask him about my sister's marriage, with a minimum expense of at least thirty lakhs in Chennai; also he had a plan even to rent which hotel to make the guests stay. Our finances were not that great when we had this conversation, but I am even mesmerized today by the kind of conviction he had in his vision. In the meantime, my parents had been looking actively for a groom for my sister. My dad jokingly said, "I don't know where my son-in-law is hiding and why it is so difficult to find him," one beautiful thing that happened was my dad's conversation with my sister's father-in-law while he was alive. My sister got married after my dad passed away, but the talks of the marriage had been started by my dad months before with the same party. Even today, my sister's father-in-law says he knew just with a phone call what a gem of a person my dad was, who listened so patiently without any judgment to his talks about the difficulties in finding a bride.

When I told my dad I wanted to study M.D. after getting my license, my dad was very supportive. I remember writing my first entrance exam for JIPMER; the exam center was forty kilometers from our home. It was on a Sunday; my dad went along with me, sacrificing his one rest day despite me saying I could go by myself; he was more enthusiastic about my exam and higher education than I was. I got a chance to come to JIPMER three months later for an open round of counseling on a weekday. My dad accompanied me despite his busy schedule; I told him that so many people had come and only a few seats were available. He said, believe in God; if you have no chance here, you wouldn't even come here. I was very skeptical, though. After initial verification of documents, my dad and I visited my aunt's house, where my dad rested for a while. I got back from counseling at college. There were only non-clinical seats available, which I had second thoughts about and chose to opt out of. I called my dad and said I could get admission into a non-clinical subject; I don't like those subjects, so I opted out. He was very upset about my decision, and we returned to Chennai the same evening, but I had no regrets. He even said that I didn't make a wise decision up to two years later, but he envisioned me studying in JIPMER.

When I returned from the Philippines, my dad told me about his vision of moving to the new house my sister had just bought; then, I could have my clinic just below the flat and join the nearby reputed medical hospital to practice medicine. I had to clear a licensure exam and repeat one year of internship before I could get my license. Meanwhile, during the internship, I acquired this idea of doing postgraduation, so I didn't pursue his vision. Though my dad had limited knowledge of the process of a doctor settling in their life, he had a beautiful vision for my career even before I was licensed to practice as a doctor. I used to see my dad and wonder,

"Wow, where is all of this coming from, the inspiration, the idea of doing something meaningful and great, and above all, his unshakeable belief in my potential."

In his entire journey, he was selfless in all roles. As a son, he gave his entire salary to his mom first and got from her to spend on his expenses; as a husband, he was always working towards harmonization, never showed ego or the need to prove himself as right, he gave in willingly for good, as a father he never rushed to finish his responsibilities of making us study some degree or getting married sooner so that he can relax, but he gave us the time and opportunity to study and stabilize ourselves though he was burdened with pending responsibilities according to the society. He always said it is okay if we suffer or struggle or face criticism, but what matters to us is you both settling in a happy, stable life irrespective of what society thinks.

I believe strongly in the law of attraction, the power of having a vision; every parent must instill this habit in their children. Today, if I can believe in a better and optimistic future despite my sudden loss, it is only because my dad taught and trained me to do so. Also, the wealth, name, fame, and possessions parents leave for their children may fade away, but building strong character and resilience and the power of having a vision will help a child live an entire life even when their loved ones are no more. It is no magic; it is a skill that is developed over a period of time with reinforcement and practice and, most importantly, being that kind of person himself.

I am very grateful and glad to have a dad who motivated me to believe that anything is possible, even when you cannot touch and feel or logically sort it out at the present. He also had immense faith in God, saying, 'If it was in god's plan, it will eventually happen; if it didn't, it means only the best is yet to come.'

Our dad had a few more things he wanted to achieve in the future but didn't materialize as he passed away unexpectedly and was part of the long-term plan after retirement. I am lucky that he shared his visions with me so I can work on them in the future.

A few short-term goals were to get my sister married and me to get a postgraduation seat in the southern part of India, which was fulfilled shortly after he passed away. His long-term goals were to build a hospital in his land in Chennai and to build a twin house for me and my sister. He also told me that he wanted me to buy a bigger house than him and my sister in the community and wanted me to get married after my postgraduation. His visions have become my obsessions now.

Parents are a huge influence on their children, but somehow, because of many stressors and responsibilities, parents are more focused on fulfilling them without giving an ounce of thought that their children are unconsciously learning from them the mannerisms, coping strategies, and way of thinking and doing things which they will carry throughout their life. Teaching the future generation to dream the seemingly impossible and attain them can be very impactful and life-changing and make them more resilient to various life stressors, especially in the current scenarios of the world, which are uncertain and more challenging.

SEVEN

DREAM COME TRUE MOMENT

After losing his job, trying business for two years, and joining a new office as an administrator, several years were spent working almost twelve hours a day; Dad finally managed to buy a new house. I still remember the day. One Sunday night, when we were in the rented house, my mom and dad discussed the plan to buy a home; as I passed by, I saw the picture of the flat layout to be constructed. I asked, "What's happening?" my dad said, "We are planning to buy a house near Mama's home". As a child, I never understood the intricacies of the difficulty of buying a house, especially with two growing children and one person earning in the family; I was delighted that I could visit my relatives often and have fun. I remember the scene crystal clear in my head even today, "All four of us sitting on the mosaic floor, keeping the plan at the center, trying to understand the plan of the house, the exact location, and the cost involved." I was overjoyed because I loved change and newness.

But all of these didn't happen suddenly; they initiated talks about it and dropped it due to financial difficulties; we moved to another rented house. After a year, this matter again popped up. After several discussions and planning, the initial payment was made for the house, and construction began. The financial situation was challenging, but my dad's face or activities never revealed any.

Because of his optimism, he was more joyful about the new home rather than temporary discomfort. While working on arranging finances, he remained carefree as he had immense faith and trust in God that he would make it happen. According to his beliefs and plan, the final day of the housewarming arrived.

I still remember the discussions, the money arrangement, and the housewarming day. The first house to get ready in the apartment, the smell of fresh cement, and early morning the chanting of the Brahmin priest and the smoke of the yagna, with my grandmom and granddad performing the ritual. When I asked my dad why mom and dad were not doing the ritual instead of my grandparents, my dad said, "It is a way of honoring your grandparents, and their blessings will help us move forward and achieve greater heights." That day, I learned to respect and show gratitude to elders without expecting anything in return. My sister had her Class Twelve public exam in the next two days. As a part of the ritual, we slept in the new home on the day of the housewarming and woke up refreshed the following day.

A few months later, the house got ready; we finally moved in permanently there. We had problems with electricity and water in the initial few days, but we managed as we had our mama's home nearby. I also learned that day one can be happy despite the discomfort one faces by seeing the cheerful face of my dad on that tiring and challenging day when we just shifted to the new home.

Soon after coming to our new home, my sister completed her schooling, and talks began about college. My dad's vision has always been that the most significant asset he will leave for us is our education, and he always said he wanted his daughters to be strong, independent, and live by the principles of being good and honest. My sister had written a competitive exam for joining college, and she cracked it.

The counseling day came; my parents and my sister went to the venue as it was offline; they waited till evening for all formalities to happen. Finally, my sister's name was called, and now she was left with two options: a course with no fee but should work offshore and another one with a 10 lakh fee and with job opportunities within the city. Now, my dad had to make a tough decision on his existing loan for the new house; he made this brave but difficult decision to get an education loan for my sister and admit her to the naval architecture course. That day, I learned from my dad however difficult the situation may be, one needs to make a decision thinking of long-term consequences and make hard but right choices irrespective of the inconvenience it can cause at the present moment. A few years later, my sister completed her course and got placed in a prestigious organization with a high-paying job. That day, I am sure my dad would have been very proud that his long-term envisioned future was happening right before him and that all his philosophy reaped the best fruit he ever imagined.

A few years later, I joined a psychology course, which made my dad very upset that even if I didn't become a doctor, I hadn't chosen an engineering course. My dad always said we should be at least one step ahead of him in all aspects of life for the better. I thought I would do something that comes to me with ease and something which I feel gravitated towards, and, most importantly, in which I believe I will excel and fetch a financially and emotionally fulfilling career. I was planning on pursuing a career in industrial psychology for my post-graduation. I could easily say from my dad's expression that he was very discontent with my choice, which constantly bothered him. One fine morning, my mom's cousin visited her in my home. He told my mom that he was planning to send his daughter abroad to study medicine, and it would cost a few million if my mom were interested in sending me to study as well so that we could be company to each other. My mom and dad initially disagreed due to financial aspects, but later made a life-changing decision. I went to the college where I joined psychology as usual. Around 11 a.m., my dad sent me the most beautiful and heart-melting message I have ever read: "Dear Vinu, we have planned for you to study medicine abroad; you can inform your current college about discontinuing your course there and coming back home." I had no words to express my joy; I felt overwhelming joy as if I had been granted superpowers or was living a dream. Now, looking back, all I could see was the selfless attitude of my parents; despite having a chronic cardiac condition, being in a very stressful private management job, with a house loan and two daughters with anticipated future expenses, I ask myself every time, "How can a human being be so selfless and take all risks only to see his daughter live the life she wants and put all his trust, hard earned money, despite all social judgments such as sending a girl abroad just to study, spending so much on a girl, how can he make such a rash decision, they all will learn only by experience when they face the consequences of taking loans, etc. and a 100 more people saying all kinds of scaring things," my dad was very firm in his decision and made that life-changing, courageous, humanly impossible, selfless, visionary decision.

All I could feel was an overwhelming sense of gratitude as I wrote this part of my Superhero's story that I couldn't have asked God for a better dad and how God has blessed me by choosing this angel to play the role of my dad teaching me every day how to be a good human, a selfless human, a visionary, a brave person, a person with a heart of gold, a person of humility, a person who has so much faith in God, himself and his family. I felt overwhelming love, sacrifice, and a visionary who lived, taught, and passed with a long-lasting impact on me, a soul who will value these life lessons, virtues, love, and gratitude for eternity.

Though Dad made the courageous decision, this wouldn't have been possible without the support of my dad's boss. I also saw how my dad had earned the trust of his boss, and once I thanked him, he told me, "It was all your dad's hard work." I was overwhelmed by the humility of his boss and my dad's efforts. My dad encouraged and showed me the outside world from a young age. He brought me to his boss's house, and I learned to think bigger as I have seen what was possible by observing their lives.

This entire journey of my completing medicine was a challenging one. Though I faced no difficulties, my dad sacrificed a lot. Money was spent like water during this period, and my dad never complained or delayed any payment even once. I always got the money, books, or clothes I asked for; however, I realize that everything was at the cost of my dad's hard-earned savings and sacrifices. I sometimes wonder what kind of love this is; in this world today where every father thinks how soon they can get their daughters married after a formal education, here is a person who bets all, well beyond what he can afford on his daughters' education only to see them live their life independently and comfortably more than he did without expecting anything in return. Once, I was abroad; I lost my purse with my ATM card and the entire money.

I had just withdrawn and was lost. Though my dad felt I was irresponsible, my parents arranged another card and money in a week. The surprising thing is my dad never scolded me for the trouble I caused him, nor said even once during his entire time with us about my irresponsible behavior or the pain it caused him. Sometimes, parents love their kids so much that they forget themselves in the process of bringing them up, and their love is so much it neutralizes all the mischief and shortcomings of their children. I am glad that I experienced the unconditional love of such a parent; it is also why I felt like I lost an asset rather than a family member when I lost him.

After I joined my first job as a doctor in a nearby charitable clinic, my dad was enthusiastic about me doing consultation, and I hope I made him proud. Every evening, he crossed by that clinic while returning from his office and would say to me I saw your patients while they were waiting for you to get a consultation. Whenever any small thing irritated me at my workplace, I would complain to my dad, saying that the sister did this, they were giving tokens beyond my timings, and I needed to work extra; my dad used to calmly reply, "In your profession, you need to make service your priority, especially people who come to your clinic are poor and complete their jobs and visit you, and you should never deny the underprivileged of the service you can offer, grow up and don't complain, it is your opportunity to get blessings, not something to be upset about," I understand these words much profoundly now long after he is gone. He also said to me, ' In the initial days of your career, experience matters, so you can work even without a salary as I did, and the workplace can be tougher; you shouldn't be complaining of the insignificant small matters, what truly matters is not the discomfort you face but the benefit of service you can provide to the community and the smile on your patient's face.' Once, a patient touched my feet, thanking me for curing her skin infection; it is a precious memory in my heart. When I told my dad that this happened, he gave me a bright, huge smile and said, "It's good, but remember to keep your feet on the ground in times of success, don't become egoistic, continue to be humble, and do the good work." Having the parent give you the right advice at the right moment is essential because when you recall some memories, the lesson they taught keeps flashing along with it.

EIGHT

FINAL GET TOGETHER

A few years passed, my sister got placed in a company with a decent salary. I graduated from a medical college, became a licensed doctor, worked as a medical officer, and we all came together in one place during the COVID period. Those were the best days of my entire life. We have been in different areas after school for our education and finally had a chance to spend time together. My dad and sister worked from home, and I was preparing for my post-graduation entrance exam. Every day, I observed how hard and focused my dad was at work, constantly attending calls and meetings and sorting out complex problems. Still, he always talked to, played, laughed, and was there for us. Dad and I watched movies together, ate, meditated, and spent quality time with my family. I enjoyed and thanked God daily, and I never wanted to separate from this loving union of four of us.

My initial plan was to make my dad retire when I joined a full-time job. However, the future had different plans. I spoke once with my dad's colleague for some suggestions regarding their health, and slowly, we came to the subject of Dad's relief from his job sooner. The work colleague shared her experience and story of her dad after retirement. She said people who are used to working will feel helpless if they retire, leading to unnecessary mental issues like the one her dad experienced. Even my dad's boss expressed his view of why retirement can cause more damage, especially for one who had been very busy with work all his life. I got so biased and left the thought then and there. I asked my dad if he could retire. The one question he asked me and I couldn't answer was the loss of pay; my salary was less than my dad's. I regret not compelling my dad to resign from his job, which may have made him live longer. I had zero clue what was coming my way, and my family hardly listened to me when it came to any major decision as I was the youngest one. My dad was adamant about working as long as possible as he believed he would never sit and eat on his daughter's money and followed it till his last breath.

The first wave of corona changed the way we lived our lives forever. In my life, that period gave me the most meaningful experiences and the quality time I have ever spent with my family. Before that, my parents and my sister were separated roughly for about nine years. We lived in different places for our education, career, and job, and we planned and met only once a year for two weeks. The first wave was like a jackpot for me, where I spent seven months, the entire day with my family. We all changed over the years, but our bond and love never changed. My sister and dad would do their work from home, and I would sit and study for my entrance exams while our mom took the most excellent care of us. We ate meals together. Our tea breaks would be so much fun. All three of us would point and urge each other to tell our mom to make tea for us, as the person going to ask would get some scoldings. My sister and dad were very focused on their work. My sister and I would compete with each other as to who would walk more steps and have a better rank in an Android app; for that matter, my entire extended family was using the app, while my sister and I had a tough competition to get rank one by walking more steps.

I would never say all the days were smooth, and we enjoyed ourselves. There were days when my dad and sister would compete for the spot with the best Wi-Fi. My sister and I would complain to each other for making noise during her calls or my studies. My mom would get upset with us for not helping her do the chores; in all conflicts, my dad would be an excellent problem solver and help all have a harmonious stay. The time we had together, the way we had fun playing board games, and laughed together would always be one of my favorite memories. For years and generations to come, it doesn't matter if we had a short time with our dad. Still, we had the best experience of a dad who lived on earth.

To add to our joy, we had a baby niece, our cousin brother's daughter, who impacted us greatly during this time. My dad liked children very much; this baby niece was an asset we played with daily, watched her grow, and sang lullabies to sleep. All our family members, including my dad, looked after her. I consider my niece a fortunate child to have experienced my dad's love. This baby was an angel in our lives. Sometimes, she made us laugh and gave us an experience of how to provide love and sustenance. Every time my dad played with her, I saw him smile more brightly and the sparkle of love and care in his eyes for my niece. My dad loved my niece so much that they gave her a diamond earring on her first birthday. My sister and I thought we were grown up. We have a diamond ring after completing college; your grandparents are so mesmerized with their cute granddaughter that she receives more than us at such a young age.

Soon after the first wave, we went to our workplaces in late November. My mom and dad attended a meditation retreat in Rajasthan the following year. Due to technical issues, they had a transit for a few hours in Mumbai. Incidentally, my dad and mom had the idea of visiting my sister at her home; in the entire eight years, it was the first time my dad called my sister due to his busy schedule, and that too by chance. My parents saw my sister, had lunch, rested briefly, and returned to the airport. It was a memorable meeting of my family members a few months before he passed away.

Soon, the second wave of COVID-19 followed shortly before my parents decided to rent a house near my dad's office, which was quite expensive, to ease my dad's travel time and to have a larger space in case my sister got engaged. I used to say to my dad for fun jokingly, dad I should write a book on you named "Mint to Mylapore," telling your journey of how you moved your residence from a local area to a posh area, your trip, and the possibilities of life would inspire people. For a few days, we had some discomfort there as there was a delay in delivery of the new furniture we had ordered for the new home. I always told my dad we should have a dining table like before, as I feel unsatisfied if I sit down and eat. Due to space constraints, we gave away our previous one and ordered a new one. But the furniture supply was so delayed that we had to cancel the order. It would have been great if we all had one meal together at the dining table, but unfortunately, it didn't happen. But we had a lot of fun there too. The second lockdown had come, and four of us spent time together for the last time.

For the first time, my dad felt physically ill with symptoms of breathlessness; he visited his doctor, and the cardiologist advised him to rest for two weeks. It was tough for us to see him fall ill, and the whole time, my mom gave my dad the best care possible. Whenever he felt anorexic, my mom cooked a different food. She mashed it well, along with other fruits and protein supplements. My uncle visited and gave my dad some homeopathic cardiac tonic, which my dad took religiously. We also got him a sliding chair to help him breathe comfortably. My mom gave him dry fruits, nuts, and fruits every day, along with medicines. During this time, my dad had a routine for himself. He never wasted time. He meditated for two hours in the morning, followed by a bath and breakfast. Then, he listened to meditation lectures, slept for a while, and completed lunch. He chatted with us for some time, followed by rest, evening meditation, walk, and family talk. He signed a few essential documents that were needed on an urgent basis whenever people from his office came home. I felt so much peace and serenity just being around him. Unlike the usual sick people constantly drowning in worry and sadness, my dad was different. He made the best of his rest time, remained calm, and maintained an optimistic attitude.

One day, I wanted my dad to watch a movie explaining life's shortness and meaningfulness. Still, he wasn't interested as it was an English movie. I connected the Tamil version of the film on YouTube to our television; we watched the movie for around two hours. It was about a family man who was running behind his career so much only to realize at the end of his life the losses he incurred on his way to the top, namely failing relationship and poor health. One more beautiful lesson the movie portrayed was making us realize that we now have a choice to value the time with our loved ones. There came a scene at the end of the movie where the successful, hardworking dad, after achieving all his career goals in his old age, passes away at his daughter's wedding; even after just watching the scene, he realized that it was just a movie I tried hard to control the tears flowing down my eyes. I had a lot of attachment to my dad, and I couldn't even bear the thought of separating a dad and a daughter. Even in movies, I treasured my dad and his love. Still, I had hardly any clue that two months later, I would be brave enough to go to the cemetery to burn my father's body after his demise.

It was so surprising for me that I could not cry. I am not in shock; I am very much aware of what has happened. Now, all my thoughts and focus were on protecting my mom and sister as my dad did. I couldn't cry before them, for I felt an intrinsic need to stay strong to keep the family's pride up. That day, I also committed to making all my dad's dreams come to reality at any cost. I had this intense pain and passion burning in my heart simultaneously, and it was tough to put my feelings into words. I felt like I had lost the most essential thing in my life, yet now I felt even more responsible for the duties I had to do as a daughter to my family. It is like you are drowning in the storm, yet you managed to find the eye of the storm and stay grounded even more robust than before. I had asked my dad at the end of the movie what he had learned from it, and my dad gave me a big smile; my mom intervened and said, "She is coming to say that you cannot go behind your work all the time, you need to take some time out for yourself and your family as we understand our time on this earth is very short, instead of regrets at the end of the life it is better to spend quality time with family now," I added, "Exactly, Dad, I hope you understood the meaning of life through this movie."

Our grandmom had visited my dad as he was unwell and stayed with us for a few days. We remember how playful it was when the new sofa arrived. We made our grandmom to sit on it first and sent a picture to our dad. He was happy to see his mom smile in that photo. My grandmom loved my dad and prayed for him to return to his best health. Because of her old age, she found adapting to the new house challenging, so she returned to my uncle's house. Even my grandmom had no clue that it was the last time she would spend time with her loving son.

Meanwhile, our cousin's sister visited our home with her son, and my dad told my mom to make tasty food that my cousin's sister liked; she was more like a daughter to my dad, and they had a strong bond, too, given the fact she was pregnant with her second child during my dad's death, she had a bit of emotional breakdown too. My dad was exceptional in giving unconditional love and sustenance, especially when it comes to handling kids. Some of our family members miss our dad as much as we do because he treated all my cousins as his son or daughter.

Our paternal cousin's sister visited my dad in the subsequent weeks with many mangoes; she was bearing a child, too, at this last meeting with my dad. They spent some time in the evening with our dad; she felt awful that her son, born after my dad's passing away, didn't have the fortune of spending time with him or having his love. The moments my dad, cousin, and sister shared this time were beautiful and memorable. My cousin recalled, "Uncle wasn't able to breathe properly. He was sitting in his easy chair" because our new furniture had not arrived. She was pregnant. My dad gave her the chair and approached the gate to send her off. She got overwhelmed by his love for her and said these are the most unforgettable loving experiences with your dad. I can't even put in words what a kind of human my dad was, ever smiling, ever loving, accommodating all our mistakes and shortcomings, only seeing and nurturing the best in us, and more importantly, he knew how to connect to kids at their level and form an emotional bond. If, at the end of my life, I have a place in people's hearts like my dad did, even at least fifty percent of what my dad had, I have lived a great life.

I had to go to rejoin work at another place as COVID slowly started to fade away. I told my parents I didn't want to go back; I wanted to work in my hometown, but my dad advised that I finish my exam and return the same day as I had put my exam center near my workplace. I unwillingly left my home that day on my parent's advice, never knowing it was the last day I would see my father for the last time. Thinking of that day still gives me goosebumps. I went against my wish without a good enough reason for why I didn't want to go. Somehow, I feel our hearts know better than our heads, and I learned the lesson that I need to trust my instincts.

As I left home, my mom and I shopped for the essential things I needed. That morning was the last day I saw my dad physically. I went in the afternoon after packing my stuff, and my uncle came to send me off at the train station. Even my mom asked why my dad hadn't reached that afternoon to send me off. I had a similar thought, too, but he was busy in his office, so I didn't mind. Maybe he knew the next time I would make a trip to Vizag. I had to go all by myself a few months later, so he wanted me to be ready to face and grow up for any situation coming my way.

NINE

THE FINAL GOODBYE

I reached my hometown airport at night around eight o'clock, mentally, physically, and emotionally drained, the rock-bottom state of my life. Now was the time to face the most harrowing nightmare of my life: to see my dad lie there lifeless. My cousin brothers had some issues parking, and I was standing outside the airport when every cab person asked me if I wanted a ride. I didn't even have the energy to say no. I just shook my head and waited patiently. In the meantime, I recalled the last time my dad arrived to pick me up at the airport when I returned from abroad; my mom, himself, and my uncle were waiting for me outside, and how brightly my dad smiled at me, knowing that I would be staying home and have permanently come back from abroad as a doctor when he or anyone had any clue that he had only three and half years with me. Sometimes, it would have been nice if life came with warning signs so we would never regret not living the better way.

As I reached the airport in my hometown, my two cousin brothers picked me up. Tears flowed down my cheek as I walked from the airport entrance to the car. I couldn't speak a word to express the sorrow I felt. I only recall my dad's words, "Finish your exam the same day. I will book a flight for you to reach home the same day," I came home two weeks later after we had that conversation, not for vacation but for his funeral. We reached our home, and as I got down to the entrance of my house, I saw many people coming and going. I couldn't face even a single person. I felt an overwhelming sense of loss as if I had failed to ensure the well-being of the most critical person in my life; I thought I had lost everything in my life in a moment and had nothing more to lose.

My dad's body had been brought to our house as my mom felt he would be happy if his final rituals were done there rather than the rented one near his office where we live. I come to the entrance of the hall. There lies the body of my dad in an icebox, surrounded by my mom, grandparents, and sister. Surprisingly, I observed silence and an extremely powerful atmosphere instead of a loud cry. I saw my mom as a whole different person; she was so stubborn and didn't shed a tear in front of me, trying to console me. I saw how strong she was, and I knew I couldn't break down at this moment and disturb the stability and peace of the atmosphere. At the same time, for the first time, I saw my 90-year-old grandfather cry, saying how my dad had left us all most suddenly. My heart was so heavy, but I couldn't shed a tear or cry loud or get upset. All I could feel was my dad silently watching me if I called; my dad couldn't bear it; it would break his heart more than him leaving his body itself, so I stayed strong. I had a question in my mind that day, "I told you, Dad, I wouldn't go this time when I left home for my job; you forced me to, why? Maybe you knew if I were near you, I would have never let you go."

Now comes the talk of who would be doing his last rights as we are two daughters; my cousin brother was willing to do my dad's final rites, but my mom asked me if I could do the last rites of my dad. The image of my dad's body burning made me cry, and my mom asked if I was scared. I said, "No, Mom, it is just that I feel Dad is leaving us forever. It makes me feel dizzy". Recalling all this today, I can see how my dad honored me even on his death day by allowing me to do his final rites. Out of all the people he knew all his life, many people truly adored my dad as a human being, as a manager, a great dad, an ideal husband, and a great son. I got the opportunity to tell him the final goodbye.

The next day, we did all the final ceremonies of garlands, people paying visits, and the priests telling the final prayers. My sister and I went to the funeral home, and I felt great pride in how my dad honored me even in his death. I felt immense sorrow yet great clarity that every event in my life has a hidden significance. My dad's body was removed from our downstairs, where we performed the remaining rituals. I held his hand for one final time; I could feel how soft and cold it felt; it was as if my dad was sound asleep. I checked his eyes, too; it was expected. I tried to figure out what had led to the sudden collapse. All his chains and ornaments were removed, but his violet-checked shirt couldn't be removed. It was torn with scissors. I felt my heart ripped apart, realizing that it was the last hour I would see him in this form, and I told them, please do it with care; don't hurt my dad, please. My dad's meditation teacher gave her good wishes and her speech for my dad, saying that the passing away of such a soul was an actual and unbearable loss for all, despite the fact she had been a meditation teacher for more than thirty years and had seen several people, there was no one as unique and virtuous as my dad and to honor him, she had got the sacred cloth which we put while offering food for God. She instructed me to put on him before his body was set on fire. She added that my dad had brought up two daughters like sons and that we would keep his name and pride for years to come. Despite the pain of losing him, I felt immense dignity in the influence that he had left on people around him.

Our journey towards the cemetery began; I held the pot with burning wood and ashes inside tied in a rope; a vehicle came in which my dad's body was placed; my sister and I sat in the front, holding the pot out the window, all my cousin brothers and relatives walking at the back, the vehicle moved slowly, and many people asked me if the pot was hot or heavy and that they would carry for me, I was thinking to myself I am bearing the immense pain I ever faced in my heart right now before which this hot pot or its weight causing me pain is way too insignificant, anyways I appreciated their kindness and concern and said that I could do this. As the vehicle moved forward with flowers falling behind, I remembered the days when my dad and I traveled on the bike many times, stopping at the same signal and crossing the cemetery. Everything he said and done was flashing right in front of my eyes, and we arrived at the cemetery.

We walked down the cemetery; all my cousins, brothers, and a few of my friends took his body from the vehicle outside. Here, we had another ritual of placing the body down in front of a statute, lighting camphor, saying some mantras, lifting the body from the ground, feet towards the gate, and heading towards the cemetery. Slowly, we went inside the burning area. Many people surrounded me: my relatives, dad's colleagues, and sister. Then, there was another set of rituals there. My uncle walked with me, circling my dad's body with a pot of milk; each time they punctured the pot, I felt my time with my dad was ending very soon; I could see all these things happening. Still, I couldn't feel anything; my heart was numb, and my only fierce thought was, "While my dad was alive, he has done everything best for us. when it is my turn, I will do only my best to honor him and show respect to him in every possible way in all the rituals we did." I felt the milk falling down my pink t-shirt each time the pot was broken; I felt the chillness down my spine; all my physical senses worked perfectly fine, but emotionally, I was numb.

Now comes the final time inside the cemetery; my dad's body is placed in the electric crematorium. They asked who was going to do the final ritual, they gave me the matchbox, and the white cloth provided by the meditation teacher was put over him. I lit an absolute fire to his body, gave my last kiss to my loving dad, and saw his body going into the machine, knowing this was the last time ever I would see him in this physical form. I felt nothing and was numb, and I walked out of the cemetery. It is a ritual that the person who did the final rites shouldn't turn back and walk straight out of the graveyard without looking back. It was hard, but I did it.

Finally, my sister and my uncle got into the two-wheeler and reached home; on the way, I felt people looked at me differently, with open hair tied with a small knot in the base, a pink t-shirt, and white pants with no slippers, I never bothered while chasing external things I lost my time with the most precious person in my life. I came home, about to bathe, and people from my workplace visited me and told them to have a seat. I didn't know how to respond; they understood and left the place. I took a bath, ate something, and fell asleep. Some relatives commented behind our back that we, being daughters, broke the norm and did our dad's final ritual; some were proud and looked up to us, while others looked down on us for the same matter. This day also made me realize it doesn't matter what you do; people will always comment through their glasses of positivity or negativity, and it is not your problem. You don't need to give a damn about people's opinions.

After a while, we went back to the cemetery to get my dad's ashes, after which my cousin, brothers, uncle, and I went to dissolve his ashes on the beach; on the way, I held his ash in my hand sitting at the backseat of the car, I remember once upon a time when I was too young to talk and communicate, how my dad holds me in his hand, I could feel the warmth of his arm wrapping around me. It's my time to hold him with care, tenderness, and love. I felt an intense pain at that moment and total disinterest in life as uncertain, unpredictable, and short as life is. I listened to a song with these beautiful lines, "I am a survivor; I won't give up." Every anger, hurt, and pain I had at that moment, I chose to imbibe in my heart and work from the fire of that passion of love for my dad.

We reached the beach; I walked under the sun, my feet in the hot sand, looking for someone who knew how to swim so they could go to the middle of the ocean to dissolve it. We dug a hole in the sand, placed the pot containing the ashes before it, and lit camphor; it instantly lit up despite the wind. The person there said it symbolized the person who lit the camphor, and the person who left the body had an intense love and close relationship. It was indeed true, he said by chance. As I dissolved the small amount of his ash in the ocean, I felt I had lost all my belongings. Yet, the sound and breeze of the sea made me think lightened as if the breeze carried away all of this pain and heaviness, and the waves soothed my heart. I couldn't let go of my dad; I picked a part of his ash and kept it in a separate container. We gave the remaining ash to the fisherman to dissolve it in the middle of the ocean.

We returned to our home and, on the way, stopped at a nearby temple to finish some ritual like lighting camphor in front of the temple; every time I did any ritual, the only thought in my heart was wherever you are destined to go, I want you only to be at peace, surrounded by a loving and peaceful family, a family that could sustain you only with the best things.

I came home, after the exhausting day of my life, mentally, physically, emotionally, totally lost, clueless about where to go from there, totally upset, broken, yet putting up a brave face in front of my family members, having an overwhelming emotion that I can't even put into words, having a sense of responsibility towards my mom and elder sister, that I will provide them with the equal care, love, sustenance, support to them. It's my way of honoring my dad in return for his great favours; all I could feel is it's my turn to show my gratitude to him by living the life he dreamt of, by fulfilling his wishes, and by being a good daughter to my mom and a responsible sister. Whenever I hear a crying sound in my home, it lit a fire in my heart. It made me feel an intense need to do something to resolve the entire situation, at least by giving them a temporary distraction.

The same evening began the sixteen-day ritual; I lit the lamp at three places: one inside my home, one at the entrance of our flat, and one downstairs where his final ceremony was done. Every morning, we make the food and offer it in front of his picture, do pooja, and water the seeds the priest gave. On day three, relatives came to our home to perform some rituals, followed by one day of stay at our uncle's home. A few days later, one night, my mom and many other relatives had to stay awake for the ritual. During these rituals, one of the painful processes was to see my mom remove the chain and ring my dad had put on her during their marriage. It is a

strange and heartbreaking process to see if your loved one is going through it; for the first time, I saw my mom without any ornaments and a plain saree. It was heartbreaking for me and my uncle. Still, my mom was unaffected and stable as she had been meditating and used to wear a white saree for the meditation class.

We had to vacate our rented house near my dad's office. I, my sister, and my cousin brother went to my dad's office, got his bag and shoes, went to that house, and picked up some stuff. As I entered the house, I saw the half glass of tea on the table, the tea my mom left halfway through upon getting the call from Dad's office. The kitchen had some spoiled food of rice, spinach dal, and meal maker fry, which was the last meal my mom cooked for my dad; I cleaned all those, and for a minute, I felt like I was transported to the past since I was not physically present there at that time, I felt like re-living what had happened. A few days later, my sister and cousin brother went there, packed all our things, and transported them back to our own house. I remember, "It was raining in the morning, and we helped carry the small stuff from the vehicle to our home; those moments of walking in the rain, it was just drizzling, and the chilled breeze eased the ache in my heart. The furniture we got for the new home was all so unique; I thought for a moment and smiled to myself about how all these things were destined with how much love and expectations my dad would have ordered all these things only to have the fortune of experiencing it for a short time and pass away so soon.

Similarly, a 16-day ritual was completed, and the day of the final ceremony arrived. My relatives and I walked to a nearby hall where a Brahmin priest offered final prayers to my dad, where my elder brother primarily did the rituals. Usually, girls don't visit these places, but I did; I would do anything if it were something for my dad, even if the whole world is against it. Among all the events, my mom is the biggest support for us to be strong and courageous. All my relatives came, gave their condolences, had lunch, and left our home. All these days of rituals, we were so occupied with preparing for it now. Finally, we sit down and think of how to move ahead.

As I was sitting on my couch, one of my friends texted me, asking me how I was and if I was going to take any exams that were approaching soon.

I was surprised that I was not even aware of the upcoming entrance exam dates a week later, for which my exam center was in another state where I was working. Even before I had time to process the entire thing, I saw the next exam challenge coming my way. Now, I had to decide between returning and joining my work two weeks later or leaving home in another four days to write my exam. I made the hard decision to leave my home and go to write my exam within 21 days of my dad's funeral.

My sister booked my tickets, and I informed my office about rejoining soon. I packed my stuff, practiced a few multiple-choice questions, and left my home half-heartedly. I tried to bring my mom and my sister with me as I had a separate flat for accommodation. Still, the organization disapproved of my request, and even my family was not ready to move out. Many procedures had to be processed, like legal heir certificates, closing bank accounts, claiming insurance, and provident fund. I went mainly because my dad wanted me to study M.D. in my state; I went and wrote the exam with very little preparation.

Looking back at all those events, I realize how my dad had been so selfless, and how self-centered I have been, thinking only about me, how insensitive I had been, had I opted for the M.D. seat while he was around, how happy he would have been, and I miss him not my worst days for he has taught me how to walk straight into the problem fearlessly and get out with a much more robust version of myself. Still, I miss him the most on my best days as he was the first person I would call because his happiness and smile me makes a hundredfold happier than the event itself; my great days have become good days. I am waiting for the day I meet you again; the moment I meet you in a different form, I will recognize in an instant, my heart will feel complete again, with an overwhelming sense of love, joy, and lightness. My dad never denied any of my wishes in his lifetime. I have made a secret wish to my dad that he should be born in my home again as a tiny baby. I want to sustain myself in the most beautiful and best way possible, showing gratitude to him.

I felt the final goodbye we said to our dad was the day I started to see the reality of life as it was, began to take responsibilities, where my childish nature of being a younger child faded away, I began to take life seriously, took advantage of every opportunity that came in my life, understood the concise nature of life and its uncertainties, made a commitment to myself that I would make all my dad's dreams a reality. I processed the burning pain to passion, became more focused on achieving the goals, willing to make any sacrifice just like my dad, and stepped into the arena of the unknown with immense courage, knowing that my dad was silently watching over me along with my all-time partner, my best friend and support, my most beloved Supreme father.

Sometimes, the so-called worst days of our life can be an actual blessing; it is our life's way of teaching us the hard way, the purpose of our life, to groom our character in the most beautiful way possible, to prepare us and make us realize what is essential, it's not the achievements we make in our career, or the degrees we have or the wealth we accumulate or the social prestige or status we have, it is the memory of the great times we spend with our loved ones, for only this we will remember on our deathbed.

To all the people reading this right now, I would like you to realize that time with our loved ones is not forever; take some time to pay attention to what truly matters, spend time with them, and make a little effort to fulfill their wishes. At the same time, they are alive whenever it is within your reach, even if they don't mean anything to you. Do something to put that smile on their face, capture that moment in your heart, for these are the only things you will remember when they are no longer physically present with you.

The lessons I learned that day are the most valuable: the importance of understanding the power of now, postponing to live your dream can only cause you disappointment, always see the bigger picture, not of temporary comfort and feeling of healthy being, go out put yourself out of your comfort zone, take risks, give in your everything, the regret of not having done something within your power can cause one immense distress, action is always more robust and less painful than regret, in this present world, where everyone becomes self-centered subconsciously with mundane things, the routine job of ours, one needs to take time to give a moment of their day to check the wellbeing of each family member, contribute to their wellbeing, acting out our best interest for them, make them feel supported, loved, cared. This event made me look at each day differently; after feeling intense sorrow, I started to feel intense bliss and gratitude for each breath I took. I saw each breath as an opportunity to impact people's lives positively, and I felt even more alive; the family gatherings, which didn't mean much to me earlier, felt like the most important event. I started to live each day as it was, rather than hoping for a future wonderful life as I realized the wonder of each moment of my present life.

Some things happen to which you can fit no logic of yours. I experienced all of this, and the upcoming part of the book can give you goosebumps. The situation at our home is that the main person of the family had suddenly passed away; generally, the family stumbles a bit, slowly recovering and stabilizing over a year or so. But what happened in my home is exactly the opposite; the things my dad wished started coming together. My sister's father-in-law came in person before she got married to his son to give his condolence as he liked my sister's profile and my dad's personality of his patient listening to him on the phone. A week later, the groom's family came to our home and asked if my sister could marry their son. To give a complete picture, it is exactly forty days after my dad's passing away. We were not even in the mindset of continuing our life as before, but the right people came themselves. My dad may have been making all these things work out in our favour from his subtle form.

My family agreed, but my mom had clearly explained that we needed time to make marriage arrangements. Due to astrological reasons, the groom's father wanted the marriage to happen as soon as possible; my mom said we could have a simple wedding at a temple. But the groom's family said they would take care of the marriage work and financial responsibilities, and on day 70 after my dad's death, my sister's marriage happened. Looking back, we never really had the time to sit and vent our emotions or plan our future; all the situations turned in our favour and demanded us to take action immediately and prevented us from drowning in sorrow and hopelessness. As we all know, a marriage requires much work and coordination. We had to be on our toes, and our maternal uncles and cousin brothers played a vital role.

In the meantime, I had given my postgraduation entrance exams and was in Vizag. My sister's engagement happened, and I attended it virtually. I resigned from my job ten days before my sister's marriage and came back to my hometown. Wedding in India requires immense preparation and money, time, coordination, and resources. Every day, we had some work or other coming up, sending marriage invitations, shopping for the bride's attire, preparing for various rituals, arranging food, etc. Finally, we had to pack our things and leave for the marriage venue, which was quite far from our place. I felt like an adult for the first time, helping the bride get ready and co-ordinating people's requirements for their stay and food. It was a stressful yet beautiful two days when I saw my sister beautifully dressed; finally, it was time for the bride and groom to tie the knot. In our culture, if a woman is a widow, she is not allowed to do rituals for auspicious events; in that context, my uncle and aunt did all the rituals for my sister. However, just before the final ceremony, my mom was called to the stage when my sister fell at my mom's feet and got her blessings. It was a heartbreaking moment for me to see my mom cry on the stage just a few minutes before the groom tied the *thali*, a holy gold chain that completes the marriage ceremony.

I understood how much my mom missed my dad; they brought us into the world together, raised us, watched us grow and graduate, and, finally while my sister was getting married, my mom missed him. I always saw my mom as a strong and independent person who hardly expressed any fragility, but that day was unforgettable. This is the second time in my life that I experienced intense happiness when my sister was getting married and intense sorrow that my dad was not around at the same time. Sometimes, life gives us these experiences to understand precisely what people are going through one day. I left right after my sister's marriage to take another entrance exam. We have had some hardships while traveling, staying, and food, but no complaints, as they are all part of the journey.

I have been thinking about how my dad would have reacted if he had been around after my sister's marriage. My cousin's sister, who married a year before my sister, shared her experience with my dad right after her marriage. My dad treated all my cousins as their daughters or sons. She recalled, "The bond I and Chita, a term for dad's younger brother, shared before marriage was fun, enjoyment, and positivity; however, after I got married and he had come to leave me in my in-laws home, I saw Chita's eyes getting a bit teary, I felt his fatherly love and concern for leaving me in the new home, it was a very emotional moment and will always stay close to my heart." It was quite a surprise for me as I had never noticed this in my dad before. We had gone abroad to different states in India, and he was happy and confident in sending us off; maybe his love for us to grow and settle in life was more than the emotional discomfort of separation, which he never expressed to us.

TEN

LESSONS FROM THE SUPERHERO

The foremost thing I admire about my dad is his loyalty. I learned from him that one needs to work hard and remain loyal to the work one does. He has had offers of bribes, but he never took them and stayed committed to his work. In his entire life, he has worked only in two offices. He only changed jobs once his first company shut down. I can see now how difficult it can be to work in one place for so long, yet my dad made it and occupied an irreplaceable position in his office.

As a father, he gave us his unconditional love; he wouldn't quickly get angry at me or scold me. He was very patient and tolerant with me and the entire family. No one will ever recall my dad being angry; he was always smiling, friendly, peaceful, humble, and loving. I have never seen my dad fight with my mom, even once in my entire life. To be raised by him and to have been a part of this family makes me feel so special and grateful.

My dad was very hardworking; he never taught me the values of life, but every day, I saw him embody virtues in action, which automatically inspired us to have good integrity and pure feelings. His scores in school could have been better, and he excelled in college; he fought his way up the ladder only with hard work as his backbone, not his skills or talents. From getting past his exams to studying in an evening college while working a part-time job, he worked his way up from starting as an assistant manager to Deputy General Manager by working almost 12 hours every day, being very patient and tolerant of everything that happened at his workplace. My dad showed me the value of being patient with hope; there were days when I felt things were not going my way, and I may never achieve what I wanted to accomplish. Despite having the best opportunities around me, my dad always stood by my side. When I see him, and at that exact moment, I feel relieved of all the burden, and optimism reigns in my mind. He always told me to be carefree about the results once I have put in all my effort, especially when I cannot do anything about the situation now. He showed me possibilities; he taught me how to trust God's plan in one's life and stay calm. All of this came in handy when he left us; I cannot explain, despite the unimaginable sudden loss which had the absolute potential to drown me completely, I didn't drown in it; I stood up, held my head, walked fearlessly by placing all my faith and hope in God, trusting his perfect plan and the courage that I had my dad's blessing to cross all hardships effortlessly and successfully. Unlike the usual parents, our dad never told us to study, get high marks, learn to dance, or get the first prize; my dad always emphasized the importance of basic things. He said no matter what happens, you should eat well first, sleep well, and finally study well. My parents put us in martial arts training like karate and kobudo from a young age. They helped us to cultivate the habit of being independent, self-reliant, courageous, and confident. My dad was happy whenever we won prizes and even got a participation certificate; he accepted and loved us just the way we were instead of constantly pushing us towards high, unrealistic expectations. This quality of his has made him an exceptional leader who balances love with the law. He provided everyone with a work environment that nurtured, sustained, and helped them grow while accepting and appreciating their flaws and skills and guiding them with love, making him a leader whom his employees loved. At his funeral, I got to hear stories from other employees of the company of how he lived as a role model in various aspects, like his ability to handle a stressful situation calmly, being a punctual, sincere, hardworking, loyal, and considerate person with a kind heart yet balanced it with the authority of getting work done and pushing people to the best version they can be.

My dad was also happy; we never had to do big things to make him happy. He was even pleased with the tiniest of our good actions, even when we felt low or guilty of not accomplishing something. He had the magical skill of making us change our mood instantly, saying that you cannot change what has happened and also quoting an example from his own life of how much worse it could have been, giving a pat on our back like a signal to move forward without looking back and also I could see from him that he always had more confidence that we would reach the best possible heights of our ability and was proud of him. Many times, seeing my dad to be more confident, I imbibed it in me by default.

The way one life can inspire and impact others better than any motivation program would ever really do; my dad sparkles that kind of positivity, lightness, immense peace, and love. Despite his highly stressful job, the responsibility of two daughters and a family, and financial constraints, he never spread feelings of burden, unhappiness, or discontent. He was so content anyone near him could feel the completeness and falsely assume that maybe everything was outstanding in his life, and that is why he was sparkling with peace and contentment while being a carefree person despite huge responsibilities. It inspired and made me imbibe that beautiful quality of being content despite unfavorable situations outside. If not for my dad, I wouldn't have known this way of living is possible. I can't thank God enough for having had that experience with my dad.

My dad was a role model spouse; he was always cooperative, understood, and supported my mom. He always treated my mom with respect, showed us how a woman should be treated, listened to my mom, included mom in all the vital decision-making, and was a master of conflict resolution; he showed us how to be patient when a family member is angry, upset or vulnerable and keep the relationship healthy and contented. Despite holding a white-collar job, he was humble at home, helped mom with household chores on weekends, cooked delicious food for us, and provided a wholistic experience of a peaceful, happy, contented, and healthy environment for us to grow. He was so tolerant that he consistently showed love and support whenever a family member was not in a good mood. I remember how my dad made me laugh with his humor and instantly felt light even when I was at rock bottom.

One of the best lessons I learned from my dad was forgiveness out of love and understanding and not of compulsion. My dad knew absolutely the intentions of some people in our inner circle, which were not so good, but he was always as he was; that is, he embraced them with love every time. He forgave people instantly, saying that if they knew better, they would have done better. He was so tolerant and forgiving that even the crooked-minded people could never go against him as he bonded them with love and forgiveness for their previous mistakes. That is also one reason everyone at his funeral said how good he was as a human being, and no one said anything ill about my dad. As the saying goes, the best way to eliminate an enemy is to make them your friend. However, that can happen only if one has immense love, tolerance, and forgiveness. One can learn this quickly if someone shows us how to do it, and my dad left me this biggest asset of character.

I could recall one specific incident: when my dad was young, he saved a considerable amount before I was born. He gave it to someone for chit, something like a savings account. This person cheated my dad and many other people. My mom said how my dad responded to this scenario was just mind-blowing; he didn't curse the other person, nor responded with hatred and vengeance, but let go of the incident with forgiveness. Later, he got the news that the cheated person had gone into depression and committed suicide. My dad said, "We lost only money, but he has lost his life." He was so optimistic in a very unfavorable situation.

Optimism was a characteristic feature of my dad; even in the worst situations, he only saw and worked towards possibilities instead of drowning in the situation. When he was diagnosed with a heart problem at age 30, I never knew till I became a doctor that my dad had some health issues. He always said, believed, and behaved like a very healthy person. He had a disciplined lifestyle of a vegetarian, low-fat diet, meditation, and a supporting community. He was very positive about life even when he had several reasons to be down and upset. Every time I am upset, I recall my dad's words, "What is happening is perfect and accurate, and it will always have some good in it even if you cannot see it now; people in the world are in more pitiful situations than you are so get up, freshen and move forward and life will have many events like this, and you can't let yourself down like this several times."

I always loved how my dad looked at the world and his perspective on seeing possibilities. Sometimes, if I were in his shoes, I would have constantly grumbled about what I didn't have, thinking of myself as less gifted and not even trying to reach better heights. Even though my dad got only an evening college, he was enthusiastic and devoted himself to completing it. He worked in the morning, went to college in the evening, and paid his fees. He was always excited about education, and though he was not much supported in his early life, he gave his all in making us study whatever we wanted and never said "no" to any course or degree I wanted to have. I always knew my dad supported me in everything and could do anything. I learned from him how to help another person's dream and be a reliable one who boosts other people's confidence.

The attitude of giving to others without any expectation is another unique attribute of my dad. In all his relationships, he gave unconditional, non-judgmental love and support, was there for people in their tough times, forgiving nature; even if someone in the family has been unsupportive to my dad when he was in need, he never held that hurt in this heart and reciprocated the same way instead he just behaved the opposite by giving them the utmost support, love, care and help in times of need, leaving the selfish family members speechless. He also had this beautiful magic of changing the negative attitude of people around him to positive by constantly having a cheerful face, doing only exemplary, and being a constant source of inspiration. He always said, "You are a child of God, so you are givers and not takers." If anyone mentioned how unfair someone was with my dad, he always said, God, will always give me what I need. I don't expect anything from any human for the limited riches. He not only said those words but lived by those words till the end of his life.

Even if one has the most stressful job in the world, it is never a good enough reason for someone not to have time for laughter or spending time with one's family. Though my dad worked almost 12 hours a day, we always had dinner together when he came home. He paid attention to what we did at home, how we behaved, how we ate, and groomed us in all these aspects. On the days I behaved disrespectfully and adamantly, my dad showed me more love. He used to patiently tell the little me that I should not act that way and what I should do in those situations. He would instantly change my perspective of the situation, and I would go from crying to calm down suddenly, feel complete, and almost forget why I cried in the first place.

My dad always taught us the importance of good communication. Whenever we went out, my dad dropped me down from his bike and let me inquire about something from an unknown person under his supervision. That gave me the confidence to approach unfamiliar people, keep calm while talking, and get things done. I also felt essential and responsible enough as my parents believed in me that I could help them somehow. I used to feel very good whenever I got a task done this way. It helped to raise my self-esteem that I can do new things with confidence, poise, and calmness.

One virtue that is most important and makes you feel complete is contentment. My dad inspired me in this aspect; I never saw him discontent about anything in his life, though he had several reasons to be so. Every time I used to ask myself, I have everything in my life without much hard work or failure. Yet, I am grumbling about the minor things not going my way; my dad, on the other hand, constantly faces unfavorable situations, be it in their work. How does he maintain his calmness and contentment in all these situations? It was very intrinsic in him to accommodate or face any problem that could disturb his peace; he mastered it, changed the entire situation with his kindness and calmness, with the virtue of patience and tolerance, and remained unaffected by anything that had a potential to make him discontented. Whenever I feel nothing is going my way, I think of my dad for a second and instantly feel that I can get over all these easily; of course, I am the daughter of Vijayakumar. Suppose my dad has crossed a more stressful situation while being content. In that case, this situation is nothing for me, and I copy my dad's strategy in any condition.

Confidence is an important skill to excel in any field. My dad was very confident, even when he couldn't speak English properly when he initially joined a company as an assistant manager; he was confident in saying the words he knew and developed himself, and both the bosses he worked for didn't know our mother tongue. My dad spoke until he mastered the language, not taking negative comments from others or thinking what people would think; he was always like, if I need to get my work done, I need to speak English, he did it with confidence. He became the closest employee to both his north Indian bosses. Had he been like many others who feel shy to talk, not reaching out to people to develop his skills, he would have never reached the heights he got in his career.

Have faith and hope even when you can't see that light in your life; all of us would come across this statement. I saw my dad live this statement. Given his health, skills, and job, he had no reason to believe that he could pay in lakhs to give education to his daughters or buy a house of his own. He lived one day at a time, even if anyone around him said, "You have two daughters, how are you going to get them married, etc." my dad saw us as an absolute blessing and not a responsibility. He handled us like the most precious gift he got in his life and nurtured us emotionally and physically by getting us admission to one of the top schools in the city. He believed in us and that we would excel in our respective fields, and he would do all he could to make us succeed with flying colors, and he did the same.

Integrity is something that helps to keep one's inner peace and makes someone a trustworthy person. My dad projected himself to the outer world as he was inside. He never had hidden motives, falsely pretending for an external benefit or to please others. He constantly communicated transparently with all around him; he never withheld from saying what is the truth, even though it could have (temporary) adverse consequences. When his boss was not in a good mood, and everyone was afraid to face him, my dad used to go to his boss, keep things accurate, however harsh the truth may seem, even if it had the potential to make his boss feel a bit upset, he always did the right thing at the right time without pretending to be something he is not. I learned from him how important it is to keep one's integrity even during tough times and how it can help you gain the trust of people around you when tough times are gone. Even though having integrity may cause trouble sometimes, it makes one more reliable and trustworthy. My dad taught me the importance of this and always expected us to show integrity, especially when things are not going right. He showed us more support even when I had done something wrong as long I didn't pretend or try to hide it.

Another interesting perspective of my dad was about money. However, my dad worked hard to earn money; he was never greedy. He taught us relationships are more important than money. He also said God would provide you with what you need at the right time, so don't think of money first in anything you do. Be it a profession, think of how to deliver the best service possible, and money will follow. Also, try to gain experience and excel in your work rather than being calculative at each step.

Regarding friends, you shouldn't get into fights or become like a miser when it comes to money, but be a giver without expecting anything in return as long as you hang out with the right people. He also mentioned earning money is a necessity. Still, you shouldn't get obsessed with money as you go up the ladder; at the end of the day, you don't need a million to eat three times a day, provide for the family, have a decent place to stay, have good clothes to wear, most of the necessities don't require you to be rich, so always prioritize what is necessary like your health, relationship, education, service before money.

Being cheerful in any circumstance is a real blessing. Whenever my dad came back from work, despite his daily challenges, he was in administration, which dealt with many people and financial issues; when he saw us, he always smiled brightly. Years later, I realized that a smile always doesn't mean everything was perfect that day. Still, it is an attitude one consciously chooses to live by despite the challenging situations outside. My dad was happy and spread joy even with little things; it didn't take me more to make him happy; just funnily speaking to each other made my dad smile so brightly; even when I got something eatable like savory, he was very much delighted by it; moreover, he didn't need a more extensive or expensive thing or event to make him excited and become cheerful. Whenever my dad was around, I smiled and sometimes laughed my lungs out when our sister joined us. It was all over simple talks or seemingly insignificant things. Some of my precious memories of him now were not based on extraordinary or expensive things or events but are surprisingly daily mundane talks or things.

Nature beautifully expresses persistence, where the delicate water runs through the rock and leaves a path not because of its corrosive nature but because of constant flow over the years. There was a time when my dad lost his first job as his company was shut down. My dad was persistent; he tried several businesses like candle making, mushroom harvest, and MLM. He also upgraded his skills, like finishing a computer course and becoming a certified reiki practitioner. He almost hustled for two years to get his next job. But I have never seen my dad upset, losing hope, or getting angry. He persisted and upgraded himself till he got what he wanted. I learned from my dad no matter how hard it may look when things are not in your favor; it is never an excuse for you not to persevere and lay back, but an opportunity to develop yourself so much that the success you want cannot reject you.

Cleanliness is next to Godliness, a famous hearing we would have heard from childhood. From a very young age, my dad emphasized the importance of cleanliness and hygiene. He always showed a stern eye on days we ate without bathing in the morning. Whatever he did, be it simple household chores, he ensured everything was adequately cleaned; he would do it himself and show me, especially during the pooja days. He also emphasized wearing clean, neatly pressed clothes, tidy shoes, and well-groomed hair. He told us it's OK if you don't wear expensive things, but you should be clean and neat whatever you choose to wear. He was greatly intolerant to uncleanliness; our cupboards must be routinely cleaned, and we can only miss a bath once we are sick. He mentioned that being clean is one of the most significant factors in leading a healthy life.

My dad was a spiritual person right from a young age; he had the habit of visiting temples regularly and having his favorite deity. I remember my dad saying, "This diety is my friend and how much he enjoyed visiting this temple. In later years, he learned meditation, followed a vegetarian diet, went to meditation classes regularly, and got us with him. He meditated for almost 2 hours every day, even on the day he passed away, had a simple lifestyle and practiced whatever his meditation teacher taught; he always had the vibe of a gentle, calm, peaceful person. His doctor once said, "I don't know if it is your meditation or my medication; Vijayakumar is a living miracle." He was living proof of overcoming his physical illness through a healthy lifestyle and a powerful mindset. He told me on the days I am ill, "The body may be ill, but your mind should be powerful and healthy even when your body has some illness." He lived by the same; even up to the last day, there wasn't even a single sign of him being sick or unwell.

Though my dad didn't have the best of everything, he never complained about anything in his life; he always had a perspective of seeing the best in every situation, and he had an abundant mindset that he believed firmly that his health was excellent as solid as a rock. However, he only had a small amount of money in his wallet; he always chose only the best and royal for us, be it in clothes, accessories, or education. He had this beautiful quality of transforming any situation he had to face. If he struggled at his job, he made sure we were so educated that we got to choose our bosses rather than the compulsion of doing a job, which makes one feel stressed and worried. If he supported himself financially for college, he paid millions for my college education. He always made me believe in having an abundance of everything, be it a house, salary, happiness, or peace. Whenever I saw my dad, I felt nothing is lacking in one's life if one had the mindset of abundance internally, irrespective of the external situation, which the universe will reciprocate one day externally.

A fancy degree from a reputed college doesn't make one truly educated. Not all highly qualified individuals are wise, and the less educated are genuinely fools. Though my dad had a bachelor's in commerce and a diploma in administration and labor law, his wisdom set him apart in his career. He had ten years of experience managing people even before he was 30. He used his knowledge and insight from his books and his experience and understanding of working in a company. My dad advised me in the initial part of my career when I had just graduated, "You need to have valuable experience, not just a paycheck with no individual learning and improving one's skills. That struck me hard; one of the main reasons I started my first job was to work for a charitable clinic rather than a corporate hospital. He emphasized competence by practicing a skill long enough, learning daily to modify one's approach to each problem, internalizing knowledge, and using it at the right moment rather than just memorizing a book and going purely by expertise.

As we all know, all parents sacrifice a lot for their children to flourish. When I understood my parents' sacrifices behind our very comfortable life, I understood the selfless nature of my parents and how I am forever in debt to their love and selflessness. If I were ever in my dad's position, I would have never done what he has done, knowing that he has a health condition; he never thought of having a retirement fund and retiring sooner but investing every penny he had in securing our future. My mom's sacrifices are also innumerable, and I must write a book about her. Being selfless even in his career was surprising; he always looked for what was best for his employees and never feared looking bad in his boss's eyes as long as he knew he was doing what served justice for all. Whenever he had a better opportunity, he never chose to leave his company, with gratitude for his boss and being selfless about his time, energy, and money.

My dad showed us the virtue of self-control in every aspect of his life. He had absolute mastery over his emotions, especially anger. Can you imagine he never fought with my mom in 29 years of marriage? Until I grew up much older, my concept of marriage and husband-wife relationship was loving, harmonious, supportive, and standing up for each other while nurturing the kids. Later, I realized not all marriages are like what I see inside my home. My dad and mom were transparent in their communication, and neither had a secret. My dad also showed tremendous self-control in his eating habits, like going from a complete non-vegetarian to a low-fat, low-salt vegetarian diet with no onion and garlic.

One of the essential reasons for his unimaginable levels of self-control is his daily practice of meditation. He never got tempted by anything and will do only what bears lifelong fruit rather than temporary pleasure. He didn't spend money on entertainment, roaming, or partying with friends. However, he had the contacts and every reason to socialize. Our dad never restrained us from having fun, having the food we liked, or being lazy at times; he always mentioned the term implication of anything we did. One of the last pieces of advice my dad gave was, "Don't spend money blindly in shopping because you got paid sufficient right from the start, you don't understand the value of money, start saving." this keeps echoing in my mind time to time each time I do online shopping especially.

If one is clear where one wants to go, one can be focused and reach his destiny. My dad had absolute clarity of what he wanted; he was very focused on his work. He wanted his children to be independent, intelligent, well-educated, and in a position of power so they could decide for themselves what they wanted in life rather than leaving their destiny to fate or dependent on another human being. While having this clarity of thought, he aligned his actions towards the same; we exactly turned out to be what he mainly wanted because of my dad's clarity in his thoughts and focused efforts in making us learn self-defense, a study in the best of schools and colleges and thereby employed in prime institutions. I learned from my dad that if I wanted to accomplish what he achieved, I needed absolute clarity of the distant future and conscious effort.

One funny side of my dad is his playfulness; at times, he stooped down to our level and played with us. He played ludo with us, competing for the most comfortable spot in our home where Wi-Fi is at its best, peek-a-boo with our niece and nephew, making them laugh their lungs out by tickling; he embraced them with so much love that we had utmost fun whenever we got together, he was more of an atypical dad, not serious-faced, closed or strict, instead, he always smiled, made us laugh with his funny jokes especially when he knew I was not in my best mood, treated us as equals whenever a decision has to be made, and had the tact of conveying difficult talks funnily, sometimes he had pointed out that I shouldn't have so much ego, and be humble, he smilingly put it most adorably, "See dear, people who had been egoistic never reached anywhere in their life," followed by some funny actions, that I agreed to what he said and couldn't stop laughing about his comic action. Some may not even believe or understand how a person with a position at his job is so humble at home, makes everyone feel loved and worthy, and makes them laugh. My dad and I had both hilariously danced to a song and have the video; I am drowned by laughter whenever I see it. He was a balance of profound intelligence yet simple behavior. He was and is my superhero. He was a combination of the best things, yet he never forgot the value of simple acts of love, kindness, and happiness, which spread joy every time he was with us.

One of the attributes of earning the trust of many people around one is being straightforward. My dad never feared anyone; he was direct in what he said and did, be it in front of his strict dad, boss, or anyone he encountered. He never deceived himself into being someone he was not and was very transparent and direct in his relationships and career. He found it hard to forgive someone pretentious. This made him a trustworthy family member, employee, and boss to his subordinates. He never spoke evil things about people behind their backs, had poor tolerance for gossip, and inspired us to do the same. Though it takes a lot of courage to confront an angry boss about the actual reality of the office, however displeasing it may be, my dad always stood by his values rather than temporary instability as long as it was done for the good of many. There were stories I have heard from my grandmom of how my dad used to be open and say about his likes and dislikes about his food in front of my authoritative and angry grandfather at a very young age, finally eating only what he liked irrespective of the harsh scolding from my grandfather. I said, "Wow, that must have required a lot of courage to show integrity, especially when young and vulnerable at that tender age."

A good father becomes a great father not only by his unconditional love and sustenance but also by being economical to provide us with the life we have today. Though he was the single earning member of the family, he gave all the money to my mom and before his marriage to my grandmom. He never spent a single penny on his own. He never went shopping to buy things or clothes for himself. Instead, he entrusted everything to my mom. Even today, looking back, everything in one's life is meant to be for a reason; we were able to face and manage the finances even in his absence, as my mom is very familiar with the financial aspects of our home. My mom used to buy clothes for my dad once a year, and they both had a very economical life. The fruit of the virtue of economy of my mom and dad has reaped the fruit of financial freedom for me and my sister today. My dad is my role model as I spend money instinctively, and I understand it is an art that needs to be constantly practiced.

My dad loved having people around him and cared for our guests in our home with great food, a happy environment, and quality time. He was keen on sharing any exceptional food we had in our home with my aunt, neighbor, or guests even before we ate. He probably grew these skills of sharing and hospitality by seeing my grandmom, who regularly had guests in their home and is known for her hospitality and great food. My dad loved treating all our home guests with utmost respect, good food, and a happy environment. We learned from him that whatever little one has, it is never enough reason not to show hospitality to friends and family.

You may not need a huge success or event to show your appreciation. I saw my dad demonstrate appreciation for even tiny things that we accomplished in our lives. He was pleased and proud when we brought home even certification of participation. He liked to save our certificates in a folder and valued them dearly. At a younger age, it helped to raise our self-esteem of being good enough. We received appreciation for even more minor things, such as eating correctly, tying our shoelaces perfectly, and being obedient to smaller tasks. We didn't need to work harder to impress our dad, who embraced us with love and acceptance even for our most minor endeavors. It is also a skill he used to grow his employees by showing and acknowledging them for their excellent work and motivating them to do their best work, unlike most people who we see in the world who are in a position of power, being cynical and critical about their employees pretty much all the time, my dad was quite the opposite, he had the perfect balance of love and law when it comes to being a boss.

When faced with a troublesome situation, three types of behavior are observed in people: reacting, running away, or responding. Most of us choose the first two options; my dad always chooses the third option of responding assertively. I have seen my dad in action whenever it came to delicate matters like the partition of assets among family members or issues within the home when each one has a conflicting opinion or resolving a pay issue with a third party or between laborers and management; he was steadfast in saying what he felt was right, as politely and respectfully as possible. It's a skill developed over years of experience that can't be learned from books; I was lucky to have a living role model I observed daily and learned how to respond assertively.

My dad was more of a friend to us; he was very approachable and listened to even the most silly and funny things we needed to share, even when he returned from the office after a long day. My dad was also one of the few who felt confident about the sensitive issues in his personal and social life. He always kept sensitive things he heard from others confidential. He helped them resolve their problems by helping them with his life experience and sometimes helping them get additional support from the management. He was open-minded, never judged us, and was always available for me; he would pick up my call even if he were in a meeting that involved important legal matters or even in the middle of a conversation with a commissioner or a lawyer. He always answered my call and said he would call me later; every time he did that, I understood how important we were to him before his job. This feeling always gave me goosebumps. As a working person today, I know how many reasons one can have for not picking up the call of their loved ones. Still, my dad overcame all reasonable excuses with the power of his love for us. It is tough to make someone feel loved all the time; being patient and tolerant of one's behavior not once or twice but constantly makes my dad more unique and most missed. It would not be overrated to say that every day since he left us, the part of my heart that he nurtured through his unconditional love, acceptance, tolerance, and patience has never healed from being broken. Sometimes, the pain is good, which serves us to recall and be grateful for all the beautiful times we had, which turned into memories with our loved ones, serving as an ointment to heal our broken hearts.

A famous saying goes like this: "Death with dignity is better than life with humiliation." My dad lived a life with dignity; he never compromised with this virtue. When he perceived that his dad was cribbing about every penny he gave my dad to buy shoes or to go to a cinema or for his education, he walked to his school with rubber slippers with a torn base, let go of his desire to watch the Tamil movie "Kalviya, Selvama, Veerama" when he was very young and deciding to earn money to pay his college fee. For a kid at a very young age to make such decisions is astonishing, showing me how important it is to live with dignity, have self-respect, and not compromise it for any external benefit, however exciting or pleasing temporary comfort may seem. At a very young age, he also decided never to keep jewels at the pawn shop. He had seen how much humiliation one can face if one cannot pay back in time for several reasons and followed the same until he died.

Maturity does come with age, but even being the youngest of four kids in his home, he displayed more maturity than his siblings; he was very forgiving. When he even knew that his family members were not generous, he never held any grudge against them. All family members were essential to him and must be respected despite their mean behavior. When my dad's paycheck was not that great, my sister was about to start her schooling, and I was a six-month-old baby; his parents decided to keep him in a separate house without taking my dad's opinion if it was OK with him because of increasing expenses. My dad never showed anger or hatred towards his family members; he worked harder with unconditional support and thoughtful and intelligent directions from my mom because of their sacrifices. One day, he overcame all these financial issues, bought his own house, and made my grandparents sit to do the housewarming ceremony. It requires a heart of gold to forgive, forget people's unsupportive and betraying behavior, be always affectionate, and show respect when you reach a successful position because of your hard work and not being self-centered. He always supported and justified that his parents had four kids and that whatever they had done knowingly or unknowingly was because of their compulsion of the pressured situations they faced and always expressed gratitude for them by recalling how great his mom cooked for him or how his dad motivated him to study by showing the consequences of not learning.

Even if one doesn't have anything, one can accomplish great things and live a truly extraordinary life if one can have the faith that one can't see in front of him and have an immense determination to get things done irrespective of unfavorable situations outside. My dad was determined to give us the best education, even when he faced crucial financial problems. When my mom told my dad to change us to a school with lesser fees when he was jobless for about two years, he never compromised; he had faith that he would overcome it somehow. Without his unshakeable faith and determined actions, we would never be where we are today. He firmly believed that anything can be achieved with good intentions and honesty if one works with determination. He became deputy general manager of his company and made one of his daughters graduate with an exotic naval architecture profession. Another one became a doctor and bought his own house in the city despite having been diagnosed with cardiomyopathy at the age of 30 years, having barely any support from his parents, having a standard degree in commerce and labor law, and no recommendations for the job, if not for his faith in himself, God and future and determined actions, what else had the power to make this all possible?

Vitality is the key to a truly fulfilled life. Though my dad lived a short life, he had balance in every aspect. He paid equal attention to his physical, mental, emotional, and spiritual health. Even while having congenital physical health problems, he did all in his power to have a healthy diet, walk, surround himself with people of the right mindset, manage his emotions wisely by forgiving people who hurt him or betrayed him, let go of negativity and weakness of people around him, being grateful for all good things in life and having time for self-development, meditation, and self-growth. He showed us how to live holistically, not just with the external success of name, fame, and money but with the balance of internal success, such as peace of mind, happiness, and contentment.

Shrewd intellect enables one to make the right decisions and, if used for the welfare of others, can be a true blessing. My dad instantly knew the intentions and type of people around him because of his cleverness. Yet, he responded to all with absolutely innocent behavior very calmly. He handled people wisely, not by harsh confrontation, but by letting them be as they were, yet not under the influence of their bad behavior. People respected him not out of fear but out of love. Because of his cleverness and tactfulness, even the person who comes with evil intentions or anger goes back smiling and cheerful. There were incidents in his office when the suppliers used to go and behave aggressively for their payment. My dad used to let them let out what they wanted, later calming them by sitting with them, saying we can give you pay only by this date as the company is running out of funds. You can go ahead and take legal action. They spontaneously calmed down and came to a peaceful agreement on any conflicts.

Good habits are hard to form and live with; bad habits are easy to create and hard to live with. One habit my dad developed at a very young age is self-discipline. He woke up at 2 a.m. to study his subjects. Getting up early is hard for many of us, but he made it a habit right from a young age because of his self-discipline. Even in his teenage years, when he joined college, he woke up at 4 a.m., cycled to the train station, went to work in the morning, and college in the evening. Even till the last day of his life, he woke up early for meditation. Once he decided on something, he followed it, however challenging it may be; being a core non-vegetarian, he turned vegetarian, and he quit occasional drinking and partying once he became genuinely aware of the consequences of an unhealthy lifestyle. He also helped us implement challenging habits, such as meditation, by being a role model. I meditate every day, and I consider this habit an asset that my dad gifted me, which helped me in all the complicated life situations. It made me think, develop my instinct about getting the most feasible and correct solution, be at peace, and create immense courage to face and overcome unfamiliar situations without losing myself. He emphasized to us the need to have self-discipline by showing us the fruit of it.

ELEVEN

LIFE AFTER OUR ANGEL LEFT

The day my dad left his body was also when I woke up to the reality of life. I realized how much I was living in a fantasy world and waiting for the perfect life to unfold someday while I was blind to the needs of the hour. That was my wake-up call to be responsible and do what is right by giving little or no importance to people's opinions. I learned all my lessons the more challenging way, but I still am glad I discovered it much younger before things got too late to change. I realized how much our dad was protecting us and keeping us free from any physical, mental, or financial responsibility and how truly a princess life I lived a carefree, happy, and enjoyable one. I couldn't have asked for anything better; the days I spent with my dad were heaven on earth.

Things get very bitter just before they are about to get better. After my dad left his physical body, dramatic changes happened in our family; luckily, all were positive. My dad was subtly there helping us connect to the right people and circumstances; it was like a puzzle put in order by fitting in the right pieces individually. A week after my dad's final ritual, I took my postgraduation entrance exam and took a postgraduate seat. A month later, my sister got engaged and married the following month. We rose like a phoenix bird in what was meant to be a most remarkable fall. Behind all this, I saw the superwoman in my mom, who faced all the situations with immense courage, made wise decisions, and took charge of the family. She became a living role model for me. She taught me how to walk fearlessly amidst uncertainty and make things happen to transform our lives to the best possible in her power. That day, I also realized what essential assets a woman should possess to be successful and unshakeable no matter what life throws at them. Education, intelligence, courage to face uncertainty, patience, tolerance, and the ability to maximize the resources left. I saw in my mom in that particular period of my life how one can sit down, complain, and blame life for being unfair or move forward fearlessly and show what one is made of and rise like a star.

What the world saw was the external success that my mom made happen, like my sister's marriage in 40 days, supporting me to get a postgraduate seat in the next two months and stabilize our life despite all the uncertainty, but what the world doesn't know that she made it all happen externally even though her heart was ripping apart internally. I learned that day that one can feel heartbroken and succeed; it's all about our decisions and the essential things we need. Feeling the pain and moving forward anyway was the lesson imparted to me by my mom.

The following year, I decided to pursue a meaningful life in which I could bring transformation in the lives of other human beings who face real challenges and are looking for a way out. I got my coach training from Arfeen Khan and was certified. I started to look for ways in which I could contribute to society. Decisions truly shape your destiny. From that day, my life started improving. I promised to be on a mission to help people get amazing transformations.

In another one and a half years, my mom purchased a three-bedroom flat in my name. She wanted to secure my future, as leaving us unexpectedly one day, just like our dad, was her biggest fear. When I questioned whether a homemaker not having much money could accomplish all these, I saw her intelligent way of bringing us up to be disciplined, responsible, and mature and how she was instrumental in helping us move forward in life.

Sometimes, losing things in the most unexpected way can be heartbreaking and make one feel emotionless. There will be accompanying losses and increased responsibilities, and we will undoubtedly face them in our lives at one time or another. That's life's way of challenging you to sink or swim; the only thing that determines your response is your mindset, which you have built over the years. In my case, I have encountered heartbreak from unfaithful people and have overcome it using meditation, self-development books, and following icons like Robin Sharma. At the same time, one should also learn to appreciate what is left, all the living family members, making a firm decision to respect them, care for them, and be available for them. Some of the worst pain can make us better by making us humble as it leaves us with profound experiences of truth that one day, I will leave my loved ones the same way and not brag about the egoistic goals we achieve but instead focus on living a fulfilling life where one is a true server to the world with their time, energy, knowledge, and character.

By saying this, I didn't mean one should constantly fear dying one day but realize and live each moment of the day knowing that life is much shorter than we think. One should completely live one's life without fear of public opinion and live courageously, knowing it's worth taking risks to have something one never had according to what feels correct in one's heart without harming others. Each day is another opportunity to leave a mark that they lived the most authentic life true to themselves and their vision.

It is always better to give it all for what you can achieve. Rather than sit and wonder about the ifs when you still need to do something about your dream. I have become a more grateful person who can appreciate the smallest blessings and find immense joy in them as I finally understand that the little things matter. I also started valuing my time, how I spend it, and with whom I spend it. Usually, people around you need to help understand or to support your dreams. Still, it should not stop you from pursuing them against all odds. When you choose to start being authentic, you will begin losing the toxic people who no longer can resonate or match the energy of the new you and accept the new you. Sometimes, the unhealthy ties being cut off may feel unpleasant, but hold on; you will soon fly in the right direction and be rewarded with more excellent people who support, accept, and care for you.

Often, being tolerant to haters and patient with them can feel challenging, but understanding the misery behind these wounded hearts helps to let it go peacefully. Remember, if you keep barking at each dog on your way, you will never reach your destination. If you are wise, you better get this quick and not waste time and energy on haters but instead focus on building your dream. You are letting them go for your peace of mind and not for their sake, and let that sink in.

Every hustle I encountered built my strength and resilience to stress and helped me become a better version of myself. If you are going through some hard times, I am here to tell you much better days are to come; hold on, take a deep breath, and keep moving on. Take the help of people who have encountered similar situations without hesitation. Asking for help is a strength and skill every person needs to master. One should take the professional service of coaches during these challenging times and experience transformation, inspire others, and make this world a beautiful place to live.

This year has been good; I had my first webinar on relationships with a business school in our state. I had my first seminar with a few government officials on stress management. I launched my Podcast on "Being the best version of you." I founded my brand, VINGRIN^{TM}, an Inner Alchemy Hub, and am on a mission to transform the lives of young adults through my programs "The Digital Coaching Formula for Mental Resilience" and "The Mental Wellness Stress Challenge." The motto of VINGRIN^{TM} is to win and smile back when life throws challenges at you by courageously fighting back. I also partnered with a private firm's CEO to build a digital product on career success. This is the same year I would be publishing my book. Sometimes terrible things happen to let the genius in you blossom. I underwent a tremendous amount of pressure due to my irreplaceable losses. Still, it made me take courageous steps, which I would have never done. This one incident was the turning point of my life; every time I face adversity, I stay positive in most challenging situations, knowing that things get messy before they are about to transform into greatness.

The final message I wanted to share with this world is that superheroes exist in ordinary form in every relationship; the person whom I admired, inspired, idolized, loved, and my role model is not here anymore. What happens in your life or what happens to your life is not really in our control; sometimes it happens that people come out of nowhere, make their way into your life, and sometimes break your heart in ways you never imagined, only for you to rise like a shining star and bring out the more robust version of you which we didn't realize. Every time you feel that tearing pain in your heart of loss, betrayal, and sadness, tell yourself the best days are coming, and your life will transform in ways you never imagined.

Does life get better by itself? Obviously, no; if you are a person who thinks that things will get better just as time passes without you making some effort, I guarantee you that will never happen. No one is coming to your rescue. You have to be your rescue; take the first step of deciding to improve your life. Kind people around the world can help you. As the saying goes, when the student is ready, the master appears; if you have a strong will to transform your life and look proactively on purpose, you will make it just the way I made it. Problems and pain are real, but your choice is how long you want to stay in your low mood and desperation. You can decide in which direction your life wants to go when you want to get up from your disappointments, worries, and problems and start building a new life with a much stronger, wiser, kinder, and more resilient version of you who will be the reason for inspiring million other lives only if you want it and wishing you to live your life to your fullest potential and glow in the glory of greatness.

The Superhero Dad

Left to Right: Varsha, M.C. Vijayakumar, Vinusha

My Little World

Left to Right: V. Malarkodi and M.C. Vijayakumar

Stay Connected And Share Your Thoughts

Thank you for accompanying me on this heartfelt journey through "Little Girl's Story of a Superhero."To stay connected or share your thoughts, please feel free to reach out through the following channels:

- Website: drvj.world, vingrin.in
- Instagram:https://www.instagram.com/vinusha2709/
- LinkedIn:https://www.linkedin.com/in/vinusha-vijayakumar-9aa809211/
- For feedback, questions, or further discussions, email me @ vinushavijayakumarcoaching@gmail.com.
- You can also join the private Facebook group: "Radiant Self:Your Journey to Success" for more inspiring discussions:https://www.facebook.com/groups/vingrinlifecoachdrvj.
- Additionally, you can join the WhatsApp group for updates and insights:https://chat.whatsapp.com/LGKYco2OBOvJzxZOeanio0.

With gratitude,
Dr. Vinusha Vijayakumar